ALLERTON PARK INSTITUTE
Number 39

Papers presented at the Allerton Park Institute
Sponsored by
University of Illinois
Graduate School of Library and Information Science
held
October 26-28, 1997
Allerton Conference Center
Robert Allerton Park
Monticello, Illinois

Story:
From Fireplace to Cyberspace

Connecting children and narrative

Betsy Hearne,
Janice M. Del Negro,
Christine Jenkins,
Deborah Stevenson, editors

The Graduate School of Library and Information Science
University of Illinois at Urbana-Champaign
39th Allerton Park Institute

© 1998 by the Board of Trustees of the University of Illinois
All rights reserved. Printed in the U.S.A. on acid free paper.
ISBN 0-87845-105-6

Produced by The Publications Office of the Graduate School of Library and Information Science, University of Illinois at Urbana-Champaign, 501 E. Daniel St., Champaign, IL 61820-6903

Managing Editor: Monica M. Walk
Production Assistant: Susan Lafferty
Graduate Assistant: Kristin Shahane
Cover Design: Heidi Kellner
Publications Committee: Leigh Estabrook, Janice Del Negro, Monica M. Walk, David Dubin

ACKNOWLEDGMENTS

The editors would like to thank Monica Walk and her staff at the GSLIS Publications Office for their Herculean efforts to ensure us of a well-produced project on schedule; and the GSLIS staff (especially Kathy Painter) and the Center for Children's Books' graduate assistants Shirley Chan, Jennifer DeBaillie, Linda Fenster, Pam McCuen, and Kate McDowell for their labors of love in making the 39th Allerton conference run smoothly.

PERMISSIONS ACKNOWLEDGMENTS

Grateful acknowledgment is made to the following for permission to reprint previously published work:

Arthur Geisert's art from pages 16 and 17 of *Pigs from 1 to 10*, ©1992; from page 15 of *Pigs from A to Z*, ©1986; and from page 5 of *The Etcher's Studio*, © 1997. Reprinted by permission of Houghton Mifflin Company.

Joseph Daniel Sobol's chapter, "The Storytelling Festival as Ritualization of the Storytelling Revival Mythos," is excerpted from *The Storyteller's Journey: An American Revival* (expected 1999). Used by permission of the University of Illinois Press.

Cover drawings are created for *The Bulletin of the Center for Children's Books* by Debra Bolgla of the UIUC Office of Publications. Used by permission of the Center for Children's Books.

Story: From Fireplace to Cyberspace

Contents

Introduction
Betsy Hearne — 1

Section One: Story as Practice
Janice M. Del Negro — 3

    Storytelling in the School Library Media Center
    Anne Shimojima — 4

    Tangled in the Web: Storytelling, Communication, and Controversy
    Karen Morgan — 11

    Summary of Workshops
    Betsy Hearne — 20

Section Two: Story as Theory
Betsy Hearne — 22

    The Storytelling Festival as Ritualization of the Storytelling Revival Mythos
    Joseph Daniel Sobol — 23

    Midwife, Witch, and Woman-Child: Metaphor for a Matriarchal Profession
    Betsy Hearne — 37

    Evaluating Stories for Diverse Audiences
    Malore I. Brown — 52

    Summary of Storytelling Concerts
    Janice M. Del Negro — 59

Section Three: Story as Literature
Deborah Stevenson 60

    Book Linking to Story
    Judith O'Malley 61

    Narrative in Picture Books
    Or, the Paper that Should Have Had Slides
    Deborah Stevenson 66

    Construction, Illustration and a Plethora of Pigs:
    Reflections on a Lecture by Arthur Geisert
    Deborah Stevenson 78

Section Four: Story as Institutional Culture
Christine Jenkins 83

    The Cycle of Story: From Fireplace to Marketplace
    Or, "The Kids Keep Tearing Their Jeans"
    Christine Jenkins 84

    For Story's Sake: Reading as its Own Reward
    Janice M. Del Negro 96

Conclusion
Christine Jenkins 106

Appendices

    Appendix A: Storytelling in the School Library
    Media Center: Bibliography and Resources
    Anne Shimojima 108

    Appendix B: Evaluating Stories for Diverse Audiences:
    Annotated Bibliography of Research Tools
    Malore I. Brown 123

    Appendix C: Allerton Park Institute 1997 Discography
    Janice M. Del Negro 125

    Appendix D: Resources for Storytellers:
    An Annotated Bibliography
    Loretta Gaffney 126

    Appendix E: Storycrafting:
    Retelling Old Tales, a Bibliography
    Janice M. Del Negro 130

About the Contributors 135

Index
Jennifer Young 139

Introduction

Stories live everywhere, but they rarely stay in one place. Despite our attempts to classify, codify, and construe them, stories keep moving too mercurially to fit intellectual categories. Stories also shape-change. They shrink or expand depending on the listener, the medium, the time, the place, and the teller. So a storytelling conference becomes an organic experience—and planning one is like lassoing an amoeba. What do you catch and how do you keep it? Or, less figuratively, what do you include and how do you preserve it? We decided on a program that incorporated both telling stories and telling about stories, both practical and theoretical approaches, both oral and literary forms, with some graphics thrown in for good measure. What's in this book is only partially what happened during the conference—a little more, a little less. The papers are revised, the tellings only described.

The first section emphasizes practical application. Anne Shimojima draws on her twenty-three years of creative experience incorporating storytelling into a school library media center. Karen Morgan describes storytellers going electronic. Susan Klein and Janice Del Negro give workshops on varied aspects of storytelling, Susan on young adult rites-of-passage tales and Janice on the adaptation of traditional tales. The second section focuses on theory. Joseph Sobol examines the storytelling revival of the 1970s and '80s. Betsy Hearne looks at women's role as midwife of stories for children in oral, print, and professional traditions. Malore Brown gives a multicultural perspective on storytelling. Meanwhile, Janice Harrington, Susan Klein, and Dan Keding balance these papers with vivid storytelling concerts. We can't recreate them, but we can tell you what they told.

The third and fourth sections move into the realm of story in book format, with Judy O'Malley book-linking thematically, Deborah Stevenson analyzing narrative in art, and Arthur Geisert storytelling the creation of a picture book with personal and professional aspects interwoven. Since Arthur's slide show eludes representation in print, we show a few pig prints. Finally, Christine Jenkins looks at stories as commodities in the economics of popular culture, and Janice Del Negro considers the story dynamic of literature in library culture.

Good storytelling makes education an entertaining experience and entertainment an educational experience. Joseph Sobol's spontaneous balladry closed a conference that proved once again how much learning comes with playing, which is—come to think of it—what stories are all about.

> Betsy Hearne
> Co-editor and 1997 Allerton Proceedings Coordinator
> Graduate School of Library and Information Science
> University of Illinois at Urbana-Champaign
> September 1998

Section One: Story as Practice

Belying the romantic ideal of a wandering storyteller shrouded in the misty fog of an imaginary past, librarians and teachers are deeply grounded professionals who recognize and appreciate the idea of information—and story—as tool chest. The first two papers to open these Allerton proceedings are eminently practical. They focus on building connections between individuals and stories. Anne Shimojima brings 25 years of library and storytelling experience to her presentation of successful and replicable story programming for students. Moving from person-to-person programming to virtual storytelling, Karen Morgan discusses information sources about storytelling, storytellers, and folklore on the Internet and the World Wide Web. Underlying both of these information-rich papers is a love of story and a commitment to storytelling that is practical as well as magical.

JMD

ANNE SHIMOJIMA
School Library Media Specialist/IMC Teacher
Braeside School
Highland Park, Illinois

Storytelling in the School Library Media Center

When a day passes it is no longer there.
What remains of it? Nothing more than a story.
If stories weren't told or books weren't written,
man would live like the beasts,
only for the day. . . .
Today, we live, but by tomorrow
today will be a story.
The whole world, all human life,
is one long story.
      Isaac Bashevis Singer
        Naftali the Storyteller and His Horse, Sus, and Other Stories (10-11)

Last year, one of our second-grade classes studied Japan. I am often called upon to tell Japanese stories, but this time I decided to try telling a story that I had formerly reserved for older students and adults. It is a sad, serious story with an unhappy ending. I was a little apprehensive about the students' responses, but I launched into it optimistically. After about three minutes, I began to notice that the room was absolutely silent. The children's eyes were fixed upon me, and the air between us seemed to be alive, filled with that story, breathing that story. I realized that although the students were staring straight at me, they didn't see me at all. They were far away in Japan, seeing the images of the story unfold before their eyes. It was one of the moments that you live for as a storyteller, a moment when the story works its magic and your listeners are changed, whether for that moment or for a lifetime.

    Amidst all of the lessons on the use of the computer catalog, the care of a book, note-taking, research, and the Internet, we as library media specialists are charged with the happy duty of reinforcing in our students a love of literature. Twenty-five years of experience in a library media center have taught me that there is no better way to introduce children to the beauty of language and the power of story than to put down that book, look our students in the eyes, and tell a story.

Storytelling is more than just entertainment, as we know. It is a powerful educational tool for the classroom or the library media center. Everyone loves a good story, and stories are the perfect vehicles for teaching and learning.

Teaching via Storytelling

- ***First, and foremost, storytelling is an art form that nurtures the spirit.*** Ellin Greene, in *Storytelling: Art & Technique,* says it best: Storytelling brings to the listeners heightened awareness—a sense of wonder, of mystery, of reverence for life. This nurturing of the spirit-self comes first. It is the primary purpose of storytelling and all other uses and effects are secondary (33). When we tell stories that have an inherent truth, we are feeding our students truth about living and about being human. Stories help us to develop compassion, understanding, and a sense of connectedness and the unity of life. Stories help us to see beyond our world into other worlds and into the hearts of other people. Stories help us to connect with a humanity that is bigger than we are as individuals.

- ***Storytelling deepens the relationship between teacher and students.*** I believe that I have profoundly changed the nature of the relationship between my students and me simply because I tell them stories. I first began to use stories with activities years ago, when I went to a fourth-grade teacher and offered to come to her classroom for 45 minutes once a week for a storytelling experiment. Over the next two months, I told stories and the children retold them, drew pictures, created a picture book, made a slide show, and did other activities to extend the stories beyond the telling. Over the course of those weeks, I began to notice that the children and I reacted to each other in a different way. When I saw them in the hallway or in the library, we smiled at each other as if we shared a secret, for storytelling, potentially one of the most powerful, intimate experiences available, had truly brought us closer together.

Children trust someone who tells something truthful. The educator who tells stories is actually giving a rare gift—the gift of himself or herself. Only you can tell stories the way you do. Only you can pick the stories you do for the reasons that you do. We tell the stories that we love, that our hearts reverberate to, that our psyches respond to. We are truly sharing of ourselves with our students, if we choose our stories carefully and prepare them with integrity. It is also a great risk for us as tellers, for we are putting out in public something that is very meaningful without that book as our crutch to come between us and our audience. But like many risks, it is an activity that is ultimately self-affirming, and we are richer for having taken the risk.

- *Storytelling enhances imagination and visualization.* It is a creative experience for all—for the teller, who must create a mood and a vision of the story, and for the listener, who must create the images and the understandings. The important work is done in the listeners' minds. This is where the story really comes to life. Students have to work for the story to be meaningful, yet it is work that is done effortlessly. The listening is active, not passive. I may select a story for my own personal reasons, but my listeners may take something completely different away—and they may take different things at different times of their lives. I cannot control what their lessons are, nor do I want to.

Storytelling provides food for fantasy, which encourages creativity, originality, and flexibility. It gives us material for daydreaming, for working out our own anxieties, for imagining and wondering. We need this imagination to survive. The information age is here, but we need more than information. We need wisdom. Stories give us the material to develop that wisdom.

- *Storytelling introduces children to literature and the beauty of language.* Vocabulary is extended and patterns of language show us the joyful playfulness of words. Using a rhythmic pattern has students immediately joining in—a decided difference from my more inhibited adult audiences! This language is especially meaningful to students because the stories are so meaningful. When I tell a story that comes from a book that our media center owns, there is an immediate rush for that book—and a long list of reserves. Children are eager to see the story in print and to experience it again through reading. Of course, storytelling also introduces students to the joy of literature even when they are unable to read.

- *Storytelling enhances reading and writing skills.* Through listening to many stories, children develop a sense of story. They learn that stories have a beginning, a middle, and an end. Stories have a problem and a resolution. There are characters and a setting. This familiarity with story structure helps students to know what to expect when they are reading, to better understand it when they meet it, and to recall it better after the story is over. Children who know story structure are armed with a powerful tool in their own writing efforts and they will innately understand what a story needs.

- *Storytelling develops listening skills.* These are skills in active listening, an experience where minds must produce images and the child must provide some effort to get the reward of the experience. Students develop concentration and the ability to follow a sequence. They learn to focus and attend, even in the middle of a busy media center.

One of my favorite times of the year is the annual telling of "Mr. Fox" to our fifth-grade classes. In the story, Mary, the main character, has stumbled upon the home of Mr. Fox, her wealthy but mysterious suitor. Mr. Fox is not at home, but Mary, curious and bold, decides to explore the house when the front door opens at her knock. Upstairs, she opens Mr. Fox's bedroom closet door to discover, to her horror, one huge vat of human hair, one of human bones, and a third of blood. She runs down the stairs only to see, through the window, Mr. Fox coming toward the house dragging a young woman. Quickly, Mary hides in the space under the stairway just seconds before Mr. Fox enters the house and starts up the stairway. When the young woman grasps the stair railing, he pulls out his sword and cuts off her hand at the wrist—a hand that falls into Mary's lap—and the room is silent and every single fifth-grader is listening!

• ***Storytelling introduces students to the world and other cultures.*** Every country has a rich heritage of story. All over the world we find the same themes of love, loss, betrayal, and journeying on the quest. We meet tricksters in every culture, as well as silly folk, wise elders, brave heroes and heroines, and evil villains. We find that we are not alone in this world. We see where we fit in to the wonderful diversity of human life. Folklore is every child's heritage—the history of humankind in stories. It is a way to celebrate our human similarities and our cultural differences at the same time.

A STORY FOR EVERY OPPORTUNITY

I never pass up an opportunity to use storytelling at school. Whether it is ghost stories at Halloween, a frog story during a unit on amphibians, coaching fifth-graders learning legends during a Native American unit, using stories with creative drama and creative writing, or during our six-week second-grade unit on folk and fairy tales, there is always time for a story. Children would rather listen to a story than do almost anything else in the media center, and frankly, I would rather be telling a story than almost anything else! But I am careful to provide times for storytelling without activities—children need times just for the sheer pleasure of hearing a good story.

In kindergarten, I start off by telling very simple stories, ideally with lots of characters but extremely simple plots. "The Great Big Enormous Turnip" is the first. I tell the story, then invite the children to act it out. We repeat the story as many times as needed to give everyone a chance (hence the large number of characters required). Of course, another option is to choose stories with fewer characters and let students know that they will have a chance to act in the future, if not today. As I am asking, "Who wants to be Grandpa? Who wants to be the dog?," the students' hands are waving wildly and they are eager to jump up and take a part. I tell the story again, but stop whenever it is time for a character to speak—and the children jump in with their lines. Having a repetitious story ensures that the children will remember their parts with ease.

In every grade level, primary through intermediate, drawing a picture of the most memorable part or the favorite part is a valuable activity. I love to see the pictures that my students have created in their minds and to know what made the most impression on them. Sometimes I give them paper that has been folded into three parts so that they can draw pictures from the beginning, the middle, and the end of the story.

Rewriting stories requires students to listen closely, recall events in a sequence, and use the vocabulary of the story. It also requires stories that are very, very short, with no repetition at all. Rewriting stories can be very tiresome if something has to be repeated over and over. Our first session is a joint one, where I tell a story and then invite the children to retell it as a class while I type it into a computer that is displayed on a screen so that they can follow along. If two classes retell the same story, I give copies of each to each teacher and invite them to post both in the room, so that students can see how the retellings produced different versions. In later stories, students will rewrite a story individually immediately after the telling. I will also invite the children to change details in the story as they put it into their own words. We discuss what elements can be changed (e.g., gender of characters) and what cannot (e.g., the ending). We decide the point of the story. What is the theme of the story? What is this story really about? The room is dead quiet as the children are writing.

Our six-week folk and fairy tale unit in second grade is made possible by the flexible schedule that allows each class to come to the media center every day for six weeks. During week one, we focus on fairy tales, with a telling every day followed by students filling out a story map. The six sections in the story map are protagonist, setting, initial action, antagonist, problem, and resolution. A lesson on 398.2 (the Dewey designation for folk and fairy tales) helps each student to find a book to carry to the classroom for the class collection. Week two focuses on Cinderella variants, starting with the classic Grimms' version. Children think they know the story, but they are surprised by this version that is so different from the Disney one, with its helpful birds, cut up feet, and wicked stepsisters being soundly punished. Story maps are still being filled out to reinforce children's familiarity with the basic story structure. Week three focuses on folktales from different continents, with notable picture books read aloud every day. During the fourth week, the telling of folktales from different countries each day is followed by an activity: drawing a picture and writing sentences describing the scene; retelling the story as a class as I type it into the computer; working with a partner to put strips of the story into correct sequence; drawing pictures of the beginning, middle, and end of the story; and drawing a map of the story, one in which the action occurs in many places.

One whole-class activity is the creation of a picture book. A long story is chosen because it must be divided into at least as many scenes as there are students in the class. After the telling, I invite the children to recall the story. Key words from each scene are written on a sheet of paper, one scene per page. Then the scenes are assigned to the children, each taking one or two, depending on the number of children. They take the papers to the classroom where they will each write the narration for the scenes. A day or two later, we gather together again and the scenes are read aloud in order. We check to make sure that nothing is left out and nothing repeated. I encourage them to be descriptive and to include dialogue. After a final edit, I type the pages. The children illustrate them and the entire book is duplicated so that each child has his or her own copy.

The final activity is the "Battle of the Folktales." The students write practice questions (In what story did a girl receive help from a fish? How do you get to Mother Holle's house?) and the teachers hold class battles. The final battle is in the media center with representatives from each class on each team, to minimize the competitive factor. It is an exciting finish to a unit that results in every child truly loving stories.

During our third-grade "Jack Tale" unit, we add on the activity of retelling in a circle. After the telling, I seat the children in a big circle and start off the story again. After a few sentences I stop and turn to the next child, who continues the telling until I say stop. We continue around the circle until the story is retold. This is a great way to invite children to tell without the pressure of having to remember an entire story.

During this unit we create a video of a story. It follows the same procedure as the making of a picture book, with each child responsible for one or two scenes. This time the children each draw pictures of their scenes on a piece of 12-inch by 18-inch paper. They write the narration to their scenes and I videotape the drawings while they read their writing off-camera. This has become one of the most popular of all storytelling activities and students are encouraged to borrow the video to show their families at home.

Our mythology/astronomy unit in fourth grade provides another opportunity to bring storytelling into the curriculum. I put up a transparency of a constellation and tell the Greek myth behind the constellation. The students will then each choose a constellation, make a transparency of it, and tell the corresponding myth to the class while showing the transparency. I've seen some amazing examples of student storytelling during this unit.

More student storytelling is encouraged during the fifth-grade unit on Native Americans. Each student is required to find, learn, and tell a Native American legend and also create a picture book of the story. I meet with the students in small groups to coach them. Two meetings per group, a week apart, are necessary at a minimum. Later they will tell their stories to younger children as they give their presentations on Native American culture.

These are only some of the many ideas that could be used to bring storytelling into the curriculum, either in the classroom or media center. Whatever ideas you choose, the rewards are great. If you've been reading stories aloud, you are already halfway there. My training in timing and expression came from the hundreds of picture books I read aloud over the years. It took only one time of putting the book down, looking into my students' eyes, and seeing their rapt attention to turn me into a believer in the power of storytelling. Above all, enjoy yourself. Have fun! Wrap your story with love and give it as a gift. Your students will love you for it.

Editor's Note: A listing of references and resources, including a folktale unit-plan for teaching second-graders, is included in the appendix of this volume.

WORKS CITED

Greene, Ellin. *Storytelling: Art & Technique*. 3rd ed. New Providence: R. R. Bowker, 1996.
Singer, Isaac Bashevis. *Naftali the Storyteller and His Horse, Sus, and Other Stories*. New York: Farrar, Straus, Giroux, 1976.

Karen Morgan
Instructor
Graduate School of Library and Information Science
Founder, STORYTELL listserv
Texas Woman's University

Tangled in the Web:
Storytelling, Communication, and Controversy

Do you have time for adventure, have an interest in storytelling, and have access to a computer equipped with a modem, Web browser, phone line, and an ISP (Internet Service Provider)? If you have answered "yes," then adventure awaits: exploring storytelling in cyberspace.

Let me give you a feel for the possibilities of cyberspace exploration by introducing three quite different cyberspace adventurers, all of whom share a love of storytelling.

We'll begin with an octogenarian from a retirement community in Arizona, who used to count among his favorite activities both mountain climbing and accompanying his wife to storytelling festivals. Today his mobility is severely limited, but he still enjoys traveling to storytelling festivals through festival Web sites as he sits in front of his bedroom computer. Four years ago, he told his son he'd never have use for a "fancy" computer and modem; now he's found new ways to communicate and to explore the world from home. He even gets his youngest grandchild involved in Web browsing. They rank highly the Web site of the *Smithsonian Magazine*, which features an article on the National Storytelling Festival (Watson) and includes colorful graphics, photos of tellers, and a recording of Don Davis telling a story. Web site visitors can either listen to Davis' entire (30-minute) story or to shorter audio clips. (A visitor who has never previously explored audio on the Web will find complete instructions on free downloading of the RealPlayer for audio.)

Next let's travel to south Texas, where an energetic young teacher involves her fifth-grade class in a unit on storytelling by having them pose questions to the subscribers of STORYTELL, the Internet listserv (a discussion group carried by electronic mail) dedicated to dialogue about storytelling. The students get caught up in the excitement of the Internet's interactivity and the involvement of people, not just from the United States but from around the world. These potential future tellers engage with their elders in the sharing of information and advice. The listserv members who become involved with this topic (or thread, in the language of the Internet) are strong storytelling advocates who appear eager to mentor the youngsters. Their teacher's enthusiasm for storytelling keeps her open to postings on the listserv of new activities and new stories for the students. In the summer of 1997, several of this teacher's fifth graders were invited to tell at a state-wide, educational conference on storytelling and impressed conference attendees with their story selections and skill in telling.

My final cyberspace adventurer is a busy Californian, a part-time youth services librarian and part-time teller, whose morning fix involves drinking the day's first cup of coffee while reading recent postings on Internet listservs and newsgroups. She often clicks her Web browser to the homepages of other tellers to see updates on their sites. Participating in forums devoted to storytelling renews her connections with others who care as much as she does for this ancient art form. It matters to her that she contributes to the ongoing dialogue about storytelling in cyber-space, and she has found herself particularly drawn to the controversies of censorship and story ownership. Told more than once that she could not tell stories that included mention of witches, spirits, or devils, this woman may click to the American Library Association's Office for Intellectual Freedom Web page or follow ALAOIF, the American Library Association's Office of Intellectual Freedom listserv.

For storytellers, story listeners, and lovers of stories, becoming tangled in the Web involves as many opportunities and ensnarements as there are interested individuals. The Internet has locations which provide recommended stories for specific occasions or projects, traditional story openings and closings, articles on and about diverse storytelling topics, and a variety of full-text versions of stories, legends, tall tales, and even story jokes, riddles, and tongue twisters. The information may be provided directly in the archives of an Internet listserv, at a particular Web site or through hypertext links (highlighted text or graphics) to many other Web pages.

Threads on listservs—such as STORYTELL or FOLKLORE—or on Usenet newsgroups (open electronic discussion forums)—such as alt.arts.storytelling, alt.folklore.info, or alt.folklore.urban—may provide stories and information not readily available elsewhere. Since STORYTELL's announced purpose, from its creation in January of 1995, was to be a tool for sustaining and supporting the interests and needs of lovers of the oral tradition and of storytellers around the world at all levels of interests and abilities, it has never been used as a vehicle by individuals who want feedback on their writing skills as alt.arts.storytelling often is. More than other listservs or groups, STORYTELL has become the "home" on the Internet for storytellers. In my informal survey of the STORYTELL archives, I encountered numerous contributions to a wide variety of discussion threads, including discussions of STORYTELL itself. In May of 1997, one listserv subscriber stated, "STORYTELL is an international association" (Miller). It is a popular and active list, often with 50 or more messages a day, and has been active since it was established by the School of Library and Information Studies at Texas Woman's University. It had over 270 subscribers five months after its creation and today maintains a consistent list of about 400. This number includes individuals as well as library and other institutional subscribers.

The ongoing and sometimes heated discussions, as well as the exchange of stories, on STORYTELL and other cybergroups may redefine what it means to be a storyteller today and could possibly be responsible for reshaping storytelling organizations tomorrow. The open and wide-ranging discussions that have been on-going in cyberspace for the past three years chart a different course from the past. First, the conversations have been free and open to everyone able to access cyberspace. Next, all participants have equal voice and equal opportunity to participate in discussions, raising issues as they see fit, not according to a large organization's agenda. Because there is no structured hierarchy in cyberspace dialogue, more voices are heard and more issues continue to be raised and debated in an open forum than ever before. Finally, the communication and collaboration among diverse people concerned with storytelling from around the world have raised the awareness and consciousness of all on a variety of issues.

Some of the debates on STORYTELL have featured "...intriguing ideas and sometimes tedious hair-splitting" (Schmidt). Discussions have covered such complex issues as censorship of stories by others and by deliberate omission, story ownership, copyright, and the ethics of storytelling. Participants have weighed in on such diverse topics as storytellers' health concerns, which include dehydration, exhaustion, and voice protection; stage presence, who has it, and how it can be developed; and the business of storytelling, such as establishing fees, using microphones, and writing mission statements, brochures, and contracts. Questions, comments, suggestions, and criticisms are raised about techniques, style, and story attributions of nationally famous tellers. Additionally, criticism has been leveled at local organizations and national associations which exist to support storytelling. Sacred cows have been discussed, poked, prodded, and sometimes butchered and barbecued. Activity in the real world has followed that in the virtual world: two years after subscribers to STORYTELL spent many months debating definitions of storytelling and what it means to be a storyteller, a committee of the National Storytelling Association took up the issue. This committee is now attempting to come up with some nationally accepted definitions. Conversations in cyberspace may stimulate and provoke in multiple directions, even providing inspiration for some to create stories or tell differently or simply to keep telling stories. (All messages posted to STORYTELL can be found in its archives, housed on the Texas Woman's University Web site, and can be searched from remote sites by keywords or downloaded in bundles organized chronologically).

Part of STORYTELL's success lies in its sustained focus on the subject of storytelling with continuous conversations in cyberspace among regular contributors and virtual passers-by. Participants say that the structured conversations have enriched their lives and acted as a powerful professional development tool. The importance of listservs like STORYTELL can be best expressed by participants. Sharon Johnson said, "Personally, I feel that it is a wonderful means of communication for kindred spirits, a way to learn more about various aspects of storytelling, a method for helping others, and a discussion mechanism for issues and ideas of major and minor importance." Elizabeth Gibson added that, for herself, STORYTELL had brought "joy in the ease of real-time communication with a number of people," and, she continued, "I can read and take part in some very interesting discussions on storytelling issues. The discussions do not always agree, but they give air to some of the concerns, ideas, and diverse points of view. . . . it is just nice to know that there are others out there facing the same lions you are." Said Lois Sprengnether, "STORYTELL and FOLKLORE both give access to source material and resource people I need, whether it's finding a lost story, or exercises to use with a group of student storytellers, or just that great on-going feeling of camaraderie that says I'm not alone." Another aspect of participation in STORYTELL is revealed in Chuck Larkin's comments: "I have been performing now for 25 years. I have a responsibility to pass on knowledge to the next generation of tellers. The Internet allows me to read current issues and to both pass on my experience and pick up new nuggets of knowledge. This provides for a rapid exchange of information with more people and for less expense then any other form of communication covering the same number of participants" (Johnson).

The reading of listserv messages goes on at all hours of the day and night: one person in front of his/her own computer screen, accessing messages, one at a time, all over the world. Normally this is a solitary act, yet paradoxically it is also a public one. The act of reading these messages deepens connections with others concerned about storytelling in the larger world. Jaye McLaughlin, a public librarian for the city of Fort Worth, Texas, explains that she particularly appreciates STORYTELL because of the "international input and questions which keep our limited outlook from here in the U.S. expanding" (Conversation). Surprising to some, especially in light of contentious debates on the list, a spirit of cooperation, collaboration, and community has developed among users of STORYTELL. Some subscribers frequently post to the list, others "lurk" and never post public messages. Yet all seem to carry on "side conversations"; subscribers send e-mail messages off-list to continue discussions begun on the list, to congratulate someone on a comment or entire message well-phrased, to ask a question privately, and much more. An interesting phenomenon has occurred among subscribers to STORYTELL: some frequently post announcements of upcoming events, others announce intentions to attend, and later meetings at events are arranged. People who have only known each other through e-mail begin to meet face-to-face; networking begun in cyberspace continues in person. STORYTELLers (as list members call themselves) regularly make arrangements to meet at festivals and workshops. Since most don't know one another by sight but only through their participation on the storytelling listserv, they wear neon-colored pins or badges that say "STORYTELL-er" for purposes of identification.

Tactics to Untangle the Web

When you get tangled in the Web, is it difficult to unearth available storytelling sites, activities, and resources? How do you keep on top of changes? Although, as professionals, we know we need to stay abreast of new developments, we also know that change is constant and remains an integral component of the Internet/Web world. Knowing how to search rather than exact places to search is of key importance. This necessitates experimenting with different ways to search, which means coming to know and even love search engines. These devices enable us to deal with the nearly 100 million pages that are on the Web today (Cuvelier 59). The sheer volume of information can be staggering. Creating "bookmarks" or keeping a list of URLs (Universal Resource Locators) of Web pages and Internet resources may help, but familiar locations may suddenly move, disappear, or become temporarily inaccessible. If the secret of success is how well we deal with "Plan B" after "Plan A" fails, we better have such contingency plans available when our "search-strands" become tangled. Since there exists no centralized catalog of Internet/Web resources available and no one single place to find what you need, searchers need to remain flexible. Search engines such as Yahoo!, Lycos, Excite, Alta Vista and Infoseek help organize the chaos. All the search engines operate somewhat differently, so spending time becoming familiar with each can be considered time well spent. Respect their differences and use various ones according to your purposes and your students' needs. Yahoo!, for example, provides results in matches divided by categories, such as arts, entertainment, and science, and includes Web pages, listservs and their archives, Usenet newsgroups, events, and more. All the search engines can be accessed for free while exploring the Web. Purchasing one or more of the various published guides to Web sites may help student searching. Copyright date is of tremendous importance; buy the most current edition of such guides as *Most Popular Web Sites: The Best of the Net from A2Z.*

Searching the archives of major universities and folklore collections can result in grand adventures of discovery for Internet/Web explorers. Let's say you want to tell a story which comes from your deepest Southern roots. Unifying the story with a song of which you only have a fragmentary memory may be a challenge that you want to take up. Your information is sketchy with regard to the song, yet you feel it would add an important dimension to your story. You know only that the song involves "riding the rails." You also remember that your mama's second cousin used to sing it, and he was a hobo during the Great Depression. You ask yourself if you can find the song, fit it with your story, and make all the components work. Can exploring in cyberspace help? Maybe. There may be an exact fit or just an adventure in the search. Try going to the Web pages of the Southern Folklife Collection, where you'll find information about gospel and spiritual songs, Southeastern blues traditions, or links to Doc Watson's page to hear him perform "Blue Railroad Train." This may work, or there may be other answers for you still to be drawn from the tangled Web of Internet sources. This approach may work in building story repertoire or creating curriculum tie-ins at all grade levels. Imagine interested students carrying out assignments involving history, literature, and music as they search the Web, constructing meaning through the text and multimedia to be found there.

There are large numbers of locations from which to start cyberspace adventuring. Harvard University, for example, maintains an extensive list of links to folklore archives, folklore journals, folklore societies (both paper and electronic), folklore publishers, information guides, and other web sites. One link from the Harvard site of particular interest to anyone working with students from kindergarten through high school is the *AskEric InfoGuide: Folk and Fairy Tales.*

Another valuable source for stories on the Web is *The Children's Literature Web Guide.* Look at its Folklore, Myth, and Legend page. With its many links to other locations on the Web, this impressive site facilitates ongoing searches. From here you can connect to folklore reference sources such as the *Encyclopedia Mythica* for information on legendary creatures, monsters, and the gods and goddesses of world mythology. Anyone interested in working on comparative studies of Cinderella variants can find links to variants of tale type 510A on *The Children's Literature Web Guide,* as well as other links to a text and image archive of English-language Cinderellas, published between 1729 and 1912. Kay Vandergrift's fine

Web site on Snow White has its own link here. Other links connect to traditional stories from Sioux to Sufi traditions, to Aesop's fables, and to the literary tales of Hans Christian Andersen.

Resources on the Web can help enrich students' assigned work. Often, school writing assignments are orally presented when they are in their final form; this presents opportunities for us to suggest storytelling techniques as a method of story creation or the use of storytelling skills in the actual oral presentation. Today more (wise) teachers are collaborating with each other and with their librarians. They instruct students in the use of storytelling techniques to select, learn, frame, and tell stories better. Not surprisingly, teachers find they are receiving better "final products" after this exposure and perhaps some storytelling coaching. Why not take this one or two steps further? Try persuading social studies and English teachers to work with students on developing and telling family stories that are infused with history-based details. Some of these family stories may be set against the backdrop of larger historical events. Focus on these stories adds value to the individual's and family's experiential circumstances. Librarians could help in the crafting of stories and serve as adviser to Web searching for the purpose of adding accurate period details. Information can be pulled from such Web sites as *The Sixties* or *The Vietnam War History Page* to become part of the students' stories. Students who want to tell of their grandparents' (or great-grandparents') Holocaust experiences during World War II should find the Web site of the *United States Holocaust Museum* invaluable. A museum that uses story exquisitely, its site includes annotated videos, transcripts of the Nuremberg Trials, photographic archives, and much more. Also effective for use with students may be an article on "Telling Family Stories," which can be downloaded from the Web site of storyteller Miriam Nadel. For the adults working with student storytellers, some of the articles on storyteller and coach Doug Lipman's Web pages may be of service.

Some teachers and librarians may want to explore connections between storytelling, readers' theater, or drama with their students. The Web can link students to theater sites as well as provide readers' theater scripts. Teachers may find useful *ERIC InfoGuides* and lesson plans for creative dramatics. Barry McWilliam's *Elderbarry's Storytelling Home Page* has links to all this, plus links to a detailed definition of storytelling by Chuck Larkin and connections to many professional organizations and to other storytellers' Web sites, which leads to more entangled links. Similarly generous in the amount of information made available is Doug Lipman's Web site, which includes Janice Del Negro's "Recent Storytelling Titles," other bibliographies, and articles on performing, stimulating student story creation, telling to children, and the coaching of storytellers. Put the phrase "storytelling ring" into a search engine like Alta Vista and get an electronic version of that old library standby, the pathfinder, an annotated list of books (in this case, Web sites) linked by theme and topic (in this case, storytelling and storytellers).

The Internet and the Web have grown exponentially in the past few years. Much of this growth is a result of word of mouth. (Storytellers, in particular, should easily be able to relate to this type of growth.) People become involved and committed to Internet use. It becomes an integral part of their lives just as it has with the three cyberspace explorers at the beginning of this piece. There is no doubt about the positive correlation of optimistic opinions among those who love storytelling and use the Internet and the Web. Their advice would be simple for storytellers, for lovers of storytelling, and for devotees of the oral tradition contemplating entangling themselves in the web of cyberspace. E-mail, you gotta have it! A storytelling listserv, you gotta have it! Access to storytelling Web sites, you gotta have it! As youth services professionals, even if you've been put off by the hype, frustrated by the constant change, challenged by the censors, troubled by the lack of access and financial strain, and distressed by the misinformation or the lack of documentation, you need to utilize the Internet and the Web to communicate, to defend your views, to make a difference, and to shape storytelling as we enter the twenty-first century. Ken Nickerson, in charge of Microsoft Network Canada, recently stated in an interview that "the content teams for the Internet... have programmers and artists, and now we've added the storyteller... [I]n the interactive world, storytelling is fundamentally critical, and we find ourselves with very few storytellers on the planet. And that's a shame, because storytelling is the future" (Randall 331).

Editor's Note: Texas Woman's University's STORYTELL archives can be accessed by the URL http://www.twu.edu/lists/ and then selecting STORYTELL from the lists and searching by keyword. STORYTELL quotes are used by permission; all efforts were made to contact participants.

WORKS CITED

American Library Association Office for Intellectual Freedom. Home page. 8 June 1998. <http://www.ala.org/oif.html>.

American Library Association Office for Intellectual Freedom. "Subscribing to ALAOIF and Other Listservs." 8 June 1998. <http://www.ala.org/alaorg/oif/news_inf.html#listserv>

Archives of TWU Discussion Lists. Texas Woman's University. 8 June 1998. <http://www2.twu.edu/archives.html>.

AskERIC InfoGuide: Folk and Fairy Tales. 8 June 1998. <http://ericir.syr.edu/Virtual/InfoGuides/Alphabetical_List_of_InfoGuides/folkandfairy12_96.html>.

The Children's Literature Web Guide. "Folklore, Myth and Legend." Ed. David K. Brown. 8 June 1998. <http://www.ucalgary.ca/~dkbrown/storfolk.html>.

Cuvelier, Monique. "How to find Web sites?" *PC Novice Guide to Netscape* 5 (1997): 58-59.

Doc Watson–American Folk Music Legend. Ed. Donna Cornick. 8 June 1998. <http://sunsite.unc.edu/DocWat/DocWat.html>.

The Encyclopedia Mythica. Ed. M. F. Lindemans. 8 June 1998. <http://www.pantheon.org/mythica/>.

Folklore and Mythology World Wide Web Sites. Harvard University. 8 June 1998. <http://www.fas.harvard.edu/~folkmyth/fandmwebsites.html>.

Johnson, Sharon. "Why This Listserv is Important." On-line posting. 24 October 1995. STORYTELL. 8 June 1998. <http://www2.twu.edu/archives/storytell.html>.

Lipman, Doug. Home page. 8 June 1998. <http://www.storypower.com/lipman/index.html>.

McLaughlin, Jaye. Telephone conversation. 1 April 1997.

McWilliams, Barry. *Elderbarry's Storytelling Home Page.* 8 June 1998. <http://www.seanet.com/~eldrbarry/>.

Miller, Eric. "Storytelling Studies." On-line posting. 24 May 1997. STORYTELL. 8 June 1998. <http://www2.twu.edu/archives/storytell.html>.

Miriam Nadel's Storytelling Page. "Telling Family Stories." Ed. Miriam Nadel. 8 June 1998. <http://www.cinenet.net/users/mhnadel/story/family.html>.

Most Popular Web Sites: The Best of the Net from A2Z. 2nd ed. Indianapolis: Lycos Press, 1997.

Schmidt, Judy. "Bravo!" On-line posting. 13 February 1996. STORYTELL. 8 June 1998. <http://www2.twu.edu/archives/storytell.html>.

The Sixties. SC Foundation. 8 June 1998. <http://www.slip.net/~scmetro/sixties.htm>.

Southern Folklife Collection. Manuscripts Department, University of North Carolina at Chapel Hill. 8 June 1998. <http://www.lib.unc.edu/mss/sfc1/>.

STORYTELL Discussion List Archives. Texas Woman's University. 8 June 1998. <http://www2.twu.edu/archives/storytell.html>.

Randall, Neil. *The Soul of the Internet: Net Gods, Netizens and the Wiring of the World.* Boston: International Thomson Computer Press, 1997.

United States Holocaust Museum. Home page. 8 June 1998. <http://www.ushmm.org/index.html>.

Vandergrift, Kay. *Snow White.* 8 June 1998. <http://www.scils.rutgers.edu/special/kay/snowwhite.html>.

Vietnam War History Page. Class project, Virginia Tech University. <http://www.bev.net/computer/htmlhelp/vietnam.html>.

Watson, Bruce. "Before Electricity, There was Storytelling." *Smithsonian Magazine.* March 1997. 8 June 1998. <http://www.smithsonianmag.com/smithsonian/issues97/mar97/storytell.html>.

WORKS CONSULTED

The Storytelling FAQ. Ed. Tim Sheppard. 8 June 1998. <http://www.lilliput.co.uk/faq.html>.

The Storytelling Ring. Ed. Kerry Mens. 8 June 1998. <http://www.tiac.net/users/papajoe/ring.htm>.

The Workshops

In each of their richly designed workshops, Janice Del Negro and Susan Klein managed to combine aspects of the practice, theory, sources, and culture of storytelling. The title of Del Negro's session, "Storycrafting: Retelling Traditional Tales," reflects only part of what she encompassed in her group session, which provided information on story structure, story ownership, the ethics of story "adoption," and issues of public domain and copyright. She also conveyed, via demonstration and group participation, some strategies for retelling folk tales and launched participants into an exercise of cooperative adaptation.

Del Negro's favorite slogan for novices is KISS, "Keep it simple, Stupid!"—i.e., when in doubt, keep your story short, concrete, and specific. She reviewed the typical compression of folktales, including a quickly introduced initial incident and selective set of characters, through a logical sequence of events with climax and efficient conclusion (no lingering on the wrap-up). Several of the groups that split up to shape their own versions of an urban legend came up with some splendidly bone-chilling tales situated in the Allerton Conference setting!

Klein's workshop, "Young Adults, Storytelling, and Rites of Passage," offered a tough-minded, open-hearted approach to teenage audiences. The key to telling stories to young adults is the attitude you bring with you, with emphasis on fearless affection, confidence, and a sense of humor. You can recognize and defuse potential troublemakers by engaging them and making strategic alliances before beginning the story. Her response to one potentially hostile challenge, "You better be good, b . . . ," was quick, to the point, and non-judgmental: "Count on it." Carry yourself as if you take no prisoners and project your voice accordingly, without forgetting that loving adolescents lessens fear of them.

In addition to autobiographical stories, Klein told rite-of-passage folktales such as "Wood-Ash Stars" (included on her tape *Wisdom's Tribute*) that focused on the subtle metamorphosis of adolescents from child to adult. For teenagers, story is "soul work, that hot fiery little thing that's aching for attention." Her view of the audience as co-creator (imaginatively, not literally; teens are embarrassed to participate in front of their peers) and her advice to get up and then get out of the story's way served to de-emphasize the storyteller's self-concern.

Both Klein and Del Negro reiterated the importance of including nothing that doesn't move the story forward—including the storyteller's ego. "It's not about you, it's about the story." And it's story that offers children, teenagers, and adults transformative power.

BH

Section Two: Story as Theory

Stories seem to have generated almost as many theories as they have audiences, especially in the academic world. Three presenters at the conference spun their own theories on different aspects of storytelling and audience. Joseph Sobol analyzed the development of the National Storytelling Festival in Jonesborough, Tennessee, as a twentieth-century turning point in the "profession" of storytelling—a movement beginning as down-home discovery and ending as organized stardom. Betsy Hearne made an analogy between women undervalued as midwives delivering babies, and women undervalued as midwives delivering stories and children's books. She also examined the role of midwife/storyteller characters in juvenile literature, who seem to reflect some of the same characteristics of professionals in the field of juvenile literature. Malore Brown described the intensely varied responses of a multicultural classroom to her storytelling course assignment on *Little Black Sambo*, emphasized how important is professional educators' awareness of ethnically diverse folktales, and told about discovering the background of her own African-American family lore.

BH

JOSEPH DANIEL SOBOL
Storyteller, Musician, Folklorist
Instructor
DePaul University School for New Learning

The Storytelling Festival as Ritualization of the Storytelling Revival Mythos

An excerpt from Chapter IV of *The Storytellers' Journey: An American Revival* (Urbana and Chicago: University of Illinois Press, expected 1999). © 1998 by Joseph Daniel Sobol.

In 1972, a schoolteacher and fledgling entrepreneur from Jonesborough, Tennessee, Jimmy Neil Smith, conceived the idea of a storytelling festival in his town. Smith's primary interest at that time was not storytelling, but civic revival. He was involved with the Jonesborough Civic Trust, a body which had organized in order to promote local historic preservation and tourism. Smith was a young, energetic, and well connected member of the Civic Trust circle at the time. He conceived the idea for a storytelling festival, inspired by a chance encounter with storytelling performance over his car radio. He brought the idea to his friends on the Civic Trust Board, offering to organize and promote an event himself, with a target date of October 1973. The Trust gave him a small grant to produce it. Somewhere in the course of that weekend, the idea seemed to take on a life of its own.

In 1982, just returned from the tenth annual National Storytelling Festival, storyteller and author George Shannon wrote a letter of appreciation to the NAPPS [The National Storytelling Association as of 1993] newsletter, *The Yarnspinner*. In it, he vividly expresses the power that the festival exerted over those who were caught up in the revival passion:

> The entire festival has become for the tellers and listeners a ritual of homecoming in the truest sense, a connecting point in the year's cycle. We return to a town we know, like *Brigadoon*, that is filled with magic of the finest kind. For the length of the festival (just as when a story is shared) all else ceases to exist. Time expands and deeper worlds are explored. It is a weekend spent surrounded by one's spiritual kin past, present, and future. For three days, no one has to explain their symbiotic relationship with stories, does not have to explain their vocation, avocation or passion. . . .The entire festival is, in ways, a giant folktale: being filled with familiar motifs and events

> that let us know where we are in the story of the weekend and of the year, that let us know we are in familiar lands and emotions, and can securely explore new worlds. And by its conclusion, the festival has become a blend of family reunion, the child's favored bedtime story cycle, and the third brother's search through unknown lands that through time, growth and careful listening, brings him back home and richer for the journey.... (1-3)

In the structure of wonder tales, there is a pattern that reflects the dramatic core of the storytelling revival, as Shannon intuited. Vladimir Propp analyzed the wonder tale form thus: beginning with a blessed original condition, there follows a transgression and fall from grace, which must be redeemed by the hero's journey. S/he accomplishes the redemption with the aid of magical tokens or helpers, which are gained by inward grace, special virtues, or by difficult lessons on the way. The return journey is again beset with trials, temptations, and, often, further transgressions which must be redeemed before the final blissful reunion and communal restoration is achieved. Joseph Campbell took virtually this same analysis and endeavored to show how myths, sacred narratives, and fireside tales from around the world tend to conform themselves to it. But perhaps Campbell's most affecting contribution lay in his enthusiastic amplification, throughout his writing and teaching, of the psychological idea that the events of each human life can be viewed through the prism of just such a mythological journey.

Anthropologist Victor Turner has written of ritual in terms that help us connect our mythic journey to the ritual pageantry of the storytelling festival:

> Ritual is, in its most typical cross-cultural expressions, a synchronization of many performative genres, and is often ordered by dramatic structure, a plot, frequently involving an act of sacrifice or self-sacrifice, which energizes and gives emotional coloring to the interdependent communicative codes which express in manifold ways the meaning inherent in the dramatic leitmotiv. (81)

I would suggest that in the liminoid spaces of storytelling festivals, where the primary communal mythos of the revival is being built, the ancient story of transgression and redemption is woven again, in metaphoric resonance with the stories told from the stage. A powerful subtext of these outward performances is the wonder tale of the storyteller herself, framed by the magic circle of the festival spotlight as the hero/ine of a cultural quest. Through the pilgrimage of the performing artist's path, she seeks to redeem society from its Hamlin-like sin of denying story and the primal unity that is story's gift. The storytelling festival became, for its most involved participants, a way of enacting a ritualized happy ending to the tale of the storyteller's journey. For the teller on stage, the festival is a homecoming, a redemption, a wedding of teller to traditions and to an idealized community. For the committed audience, the festival is redeeming, too: a homecoming to a kingdom in which storytelling is restored to its rightful place at the center of community life.

The ritual form of the storytelling festival evolved to incorporate echoes of many other liminal zones across cultures and time—the Mass, the Seder, the Eleusinian Mysteries, a brush arbor meeting, a tent revival, or American feast days like Thanksgiving, Christmas, the Fourth of July. But the death-and-resurrection story implicit in the conceptual framework of "revival" sets the overall metanarrative tone. At its heart, the revival story is a story of redemption, in which storytelling acts as a stand-in for the primal unities we have sacrificed in our journey of civilization. Storytelling pilgrims arrive at Jonesborough predisposed to believe that culture has fallen from grace. Somehow, sometime, we had sinned, by denying ourselves, our heritage, our nature, the sacred "something" that for lack of a more authoritative word for it, we would now call by the name of "the lost art of storytelling."

If we have not yet received the catechism when we arrive, the torrent of stories and exhortations about stories create a sense of cultic immersion, like the all-night chanting of the Mystery School, that immediately initiates us. The mythic pattern is read and enacted in the quickening of our spirits: In the beginning was Storytelling, and with Storytelling was Community. In Storytelling was contained the seeds of all the arts, sciences, education, politics, medicine, and law. As specializations multiplied, Storytelling died, sacrificed to the 'soulless reflections of man's skill'; it descended into cultural oblivion, where it endured as a candle in the houses of the oppressed; on the third day of the storytelling festival, by the Sunday morning epiphany of Spiritual Storytelling, Storytelling will have risen again, to return the world to Spring.

Like the medieval sin-eater, the culture's neglect of the simple communion of storytelling is made to stand in for a multitude of transgressions; and the weekend of resurrecting the art is an occasion for ritual cleansing. We repent and are absolved. "Pax Vobiscum. Go in Peace. Next year in Jonesborough." And in the center of the ritual drama is the celebrant-priest or priestess, the storyteller.

"Revival" is never about actual death—that story is too tragic and final. The key plot turn of a revival story is the revelation that death was only illusory, the result of our failed belief. No one believes that storytelling actually died, any more than the town of Jonesborough died—if they had, there would be no town, no festival, no story. These precious things are perceived as having been abandoned, turned from, denied; their values obscured by ignorance and neglect (which is sin). We're then invited to repent—gently, indirectly; we're after all most of us good middle-class late-twentieth-century adults, who would rather be caught in flagrante delicto than shouting and moaning on the mourners' bench. But by Sunday morning at your typical storytelling festival, we may have performed some of those same spiritual gymnastics.

In what follows, I will attempt a deep reading of the National Storytelling Festival as cultural text. I will examine the ritual form of the event using Arnold Van Gennep's sequential model of rites of passage—consisting of separation, transition, and reincorporation. And I will look at Jonesborough and the national storytelling revival scene through the theoretical glass of Victor Turner's "liminal and liminoid" ritual, and of his concept of communitas as the fundamental goal of ritual performance.

Speaking strictly in terms of Turner's definitions, the festival is a liminoid phenomenon: it dwells in the realm of volitional, leisure activities in a complex, postindustrial society, as opposed to the communally obligatory rites of passage and renewal in a tribal society. However, many of storytelling's most significant participants are quite selfconsciously seeking to revitalize roles, forms, and contexts from preindustrial lifeways. For these people, I would suggest that the event has had quite a different ritual and dramaturgical meaning than for those casual onlookers who have been drawn to the festival through its listing in *Holiday Magazine*'s guide to the 100 best weekend getaways. The storytelling festival can serve as a laboratory for testing the adaptability of Turner's concepts. When we do, we find that liminal and liminoid aspects are actually tightly braided in the experience and perspectives of various participants at various stages in their lives and careers.

Much depends on the individual's relationship to the festival—whether they come as spectator, amateur enthusiast, aspiring professional, featured professional teller, local traditional artist or exotic culture-bearer, National Storytelling Association insider or functionary, aspiring or actual organizer of a satellite or rival festival, or any combination thereof. Depending on one's history with the organization, the festival, and the art form, and depending also upon one's belief system in regard to the ritual efficacy of those agencies, each festival can provide various levels of initiation, can generate manifold complexes of meaning; or, it can be just another gig, just another weekend. Depending on the particular psychological necessity of storytelling and of its ritual enactments in one's own life, a particular festival can operate as a vital liminal rite, a casual liminoid episode of work or leisure, or a crass commercialization of what is already, for some, a sacred process.

I will focus here chiefly on accounts from those most deeply invested in the storytelling revival—those storytellers who treated the festival as a rite of incorporation in a storytelling community, and as a rite of revival for an art through which they were in the process of crafting a presentable social identity. I will concentrate on the experiences of those for whom the festival represented not just an optional leisure activity, but a public enactment of a ritual obligation to themselves and to a consciously conceived community. The depth and stability of these obligations and of this community are certainly open to question. Like other recent manifestations of spontaneous communitas, they were formed very quickly, burned brightly, and tended to scatter as inner contradictions revealed themselves, or as social and economic tides ebbed or flooded. I will take both sets of phenomena seriously: those attendant upon the evolution of a spontaneous storytelling communitas, and those attendant upon its possible decay.

The generalized reading of the festival below will take as its chronological reference the period of the late seventies and early- to mid-eighties, when the event was reaching its apex as a ritual center of communitas—even as the pressures of increasing popularity and internal competition were beginning to drown the serendipitous ceremonies of innocence that generated that communal spirit.

The Festival Experience

Separation from everyday reality in the storytelling festival experience begins, as we have seen, before the first story is told. At the National Storytelling Festival, paradigmatically, and to a lesser extent at many smaller regional festivals, the geographical removal of the festival site is an important element of ritual separation. As Jonesborough became truly national in scope, storytellers and would-be storytellers began to make the journey from all around the country. The effort involved became a part of the ritual and, in turn, part of festival folklore.

Many would drive together, getting off work Thursday afternoon and driving all night. Jim May would ride down from Northern Illinois:

> It was a ritual for three or four years there, when I was teaching. We'd all pack into a van. Bring lots of bags of trail-mix. And head out right after school. And drive through the mountains all night—I kind of miss that part—driving through the mountains all night. I think that's where the myth began. Those nighttime drives, with friends, and sometimes telling stories, and sometimes just listening to music, and napping, and changing drivers. But going through those mountains at night, and you'd pull off the road to rest, and you'd see those lights, down in the mist. If the conditions were just right, you'd just see that mist down there, and the lights of the towns, with these sort of mist-halos around them. And I think that, as much as anything, gave us the sense of a mythic journey. The fact that it's in the mountains is important, I think. Also there was something about crossing the Ohio River at Louisville. . . . There's something mythic about crossing those rivers, and there's some big factories there, and lots of lights. And we'd usually hit that close to midnight. So you'd be in the Kentucky mountains around two in the morning.

The overnight journeys made a fertile ground for propagating spontaneous communitas. The time of isolation within the womb-like enclosure of the car, van or bus allowed for a build up of shared expectation and commitment that overflowed onto the festival grounds. The all-night drives, too, fulfilled the functions of a vigil. Postural rigors and deprivation of sleep are traditional methods of inducing altered states. With the aid of this potent, non-pharmacological enhancement, the festival parade of narrative imagery could register with heightened intensity.

Even those who flew to the festival could find in the flight a liminal zone of separation from everyday expectations and rules. The out-of-the-way-destination helped. It necessitated at least one change of planes, the last change being to a bumpy commuter flight into Tri-Cities Airport, Upper East Tennessee—a field which could only handle dwarfish commuter jets or noisy prop planes with a dozen or so narrow, boardlike seats. Spontaneous communitas would often erupt through the natural sorting process of these festival flights. Rafe Martin recalled:

> I remember the first time I went to NAPPS, the experience was, it's like I had seen the future. You know, you're flying down on the plane, and people are talking. . . . It was like, everyone on the plane was talking storytelling. In other words, people were sharing who they were. I had been on so many flights, traveling around the country to tell stories, and they're all dead. You know, it's people buried in business work—basically going over figures and files; or sleeping; or reading really dumb books. And that's it. Instead, this was a flight of people—all different walks of life, all different looks, all different ages—and everybody was talking with one another. And there weren't racial issues, there weren't political issues—I mean, it was like, "You've got an interesting story—Neat! And then you get to Jonesborough, and you felt—this was the future. People from different political backgrounds, nationalities, races, religions—all getting along. And it didn't matter what you looked like, it didn't matter where you were from; what mattered was, if you could tell a story. And if you could, then everyone was going to be there for you.

When the time on the highway or in the netherworld of airports and airplane cabins was done, there came the moment when one turned off the divided four-lane highway 11E that runs past Jonesborough's northern flank. You cruised down a road that narrows as it approaches an Exxon station, like a gateway at the foot of a steep hill. Taking a sharp right turn around the gas station, you found yourself abruptly bumping along on cobblestones, gazing up a crowded Main Street vista that has been cunningly recomposed into a living history tableau of which you were suddenly a part. It is not a closed or complete tableau, but an open-ended collage, in which some of the dominant signifiers of twentieth-century culture—power lines and corporate advertising logos—have been conspicuously banished or hidden. Others, like autos and tourists, remain in the picture, decentering it further; and others, like the storytellers in their performing colors, and the harvest motifs sheathing the lampposts and spangling the sidewalks, make up a crazy-quilt of temporal references, in which the motley flags of post-sixties eco-gypsy culture are appliqued against a synchronic, traditional American background, with a sprinkling of syncretic, Pre-Christian accents.

Moving slowly up the street, past two short blocks of brick and limestone shop buildings on the right, past the Mail Pouch Building and the domed county courthouse on the left, then past the long white clapboard Federal-style porch of the Chester Inn on the right, conspicuously marked and dated 1797, you would arrive at the central example of Jonesborough's floating historical signifiers: the Christopher Taylor cabin. This two-story, mid-eighteenth-century log cabin had been moved from the outskirts to the center of town in 1975, and reassembled on a strip of parkland between the Chester Inn and the 1840s Greek Revival Presbyterian Church. The church is still a church, the inn has been restored through a state grant to be an office headquarters for NAPPS, and the cabin sits vacant most of the year, a mossy civic tool shed mysteriously transfigured by the knowledge that Andrew Jackson once slept there.

It was here that you underwent the first initiatory ordeal of the festival: registration. Fitting yourself into a line that straggled down the flagstone path back toward the street, you would gradually be borne toward the rough-hewn doorposts of the cabin. Stepping across the dark threshold to an interior smelling of damp earth and straw, you were confronted by tables of cheerful young votaresses, one of whom would take your name, address, NAPPS membership status, and money. In exchange, she would hand you, not a ticket, but a schedule, and a small, jagged-edged, calico swatch, pierced through by a safety pin. If you were to confess your puzzlement at this esoteric token, she might affix it to your shirt pocket with a soothing hand and the instruction that this was your weekend pass. You were to keep it constantly pinned to your person, transferring it dutifully from soiled shirt to clean, lest your way be blocked at the breach of a tent by one of the monitors—volunteer staff primed to stand and murmur "Pass by" to only those initiates bearing the calico swatch.

So, pinned and instructed, you walked out the back door of the Christopher Taylor cabin into the autumn sunlight, and found yourself on the edge of the Swappin' Grounds. If you were early enough, Doc McConnell would be there, capering about in front of his outlandishly painted wagon, dressed up in the stovepipe hat, frocktail coat, and clipped goatee of a backwoods Mephistopheles, warming up the crowds with comic patter while peddling real bottles of imaginary snake oil—an innocently postmodern genre of parody in which the pleasures of reference have been emptied of the tensions of belief.

McConnell played (and still plays, to a diluted extent) an important threshold role at the NAPPS festival and other Jonesborough events—the "greeter." As the first performer that many would encounter at the site, and also as chief Master of Ceremonies on the Swappin' Grounds,

McConnell took it upon himself to begin to induce the festival state of imaginative transport and self-forgetting. Being from the local area, he acted as a performing host, reaching out to strangers through the medium of his tall tales and hyperbolic patter. He introduced them to a rural, traditional world that was immediately assimilable, because entirely composed of inversions and impossibilities, offered up with an enveloping wink of complicity.

"Where I live," he would shout, "in Tucker's Knob, Tennessee, it got so dry one year that the Baptists took to sprinklin', and the Methodists just used a damp washcloth." At the 1982 festival he told of a Tucker's Knob entrepreneur named Crazy Jim, who opened up a restaurant called "Down Home":

> And what he done, he hit upon a bonanza. He got in touch with all them old rangers, and them wardens, and property owners, and sportsmen out in New Mexico, and Arizona, and Texas—where they have them old hard-shell armadillos out there? And they're a nuisance out there, they claim. And so Old Jim had 'em kill all them old armadillos, and pack 'em in ice, and send 'em back there to Tucker's Knob. And old Jim fixes 'em in his restaurant, and he serves 'em, and calls 'em, 'Possum on the Halfshell.'

The form of McConnell's story here is thoroughly traditional, but its content reflects the cosmopolitan system of social and economic exchange of which the festival itself is one expression. McConnell's Crazy Jim, in fact, could easily have been Jimmy Neil Smith, importing recontextualized storytellers from all over North America to small town Tennessee, and serving them up to nostalgic travelers who want their narrative possum on the halfshell of redemptive ritual. In the restored performance context of the festival, McConnell's tall tales performed an initiatory function analogous to the one they play in traditional male societies—as narrative riddles, whose solution is betokened by laughter, and whose ritual reward is incorporation into the community of knowers.

If you emerged from the Taylor cabin after McConnell's set, you might have cocked one ear to a bellowing neophyte, while scanning the schedule with one eye and the gathering flood of passersby with the other, searching for old friends and acquaintances while simultaneously straining to plot your course from hour to hour and to prepare for the coming onslaught of narrative overload. Overload is an essential transformational mode of festival consciousness. In the presentational equivalent of the cornucopia baskets splayed across the sidewalks of Main Street, three to six tents will generally be going at any given time, plus the Swappin' Grounds, and a cornucopia of consumable storytelling books, tapes, videos, and souvenirs called "the resource tent." There is too much to do, to see, to hear (and to buy) throughout the weekend, and the more one desires to be touched and transformed by the experience, the more that too-muchness pulls on the mind. One experiences the mass of festival activity proceeding always just out of reach of eye and ear as a kind of half-conscious stimulant, simultaneously a distraction and a spur to renewed intensities of receptivity.

The first formal sessions with the featured performers are billed as "Family Showcases"—lightweight, mixed programs for general audiences—and "Meet the Storyteller" workshops, in which performers are encouraged to speak in an informal, personal way about themselves and their relation to their art form. These introductory sessions initiate the process, essential to the experience of the weekend, of becoming known to one another, in the peculiar heightened way that we allow ourselves to be imprinted by performing presences in an intentional hotbed of expressive energy. Friday evening, after a dinner break, comes the first "olio." In 1985, for example, the tellers lined up, seven in one large tent, seven in another. Each would tell a 10-minute story. When all had gone, there would be a break. The little flotillas of tellers would switch tents and start over again. Audiences could get a taste of each storyteller's energy and style, and could pick their way with a more informed instinct among the array of simultaneous offerings in various tents on Saturday.

The olio serves as a baptism by immersion in the river of voices that constitute the festival in any given year. There is no pretense of closure—since the festival is avowedly constituted of all its members. "We are all storytellers" is part of storytelling movement catechism. The National Storytelling Festival takes upon itself the task of representing, not just the national storytelling scene, but a storytelling nation. It is a different nation than the one represented, say, on the nightly network news, a nation revisioned in the bright silver of the revival mythos. It is a nation of storytellers—of individuals, groups, and communities empowered by the knowledge of their stories and by the ability to share them and to be heard by their own and by one another's communities.

Before "multiculturalism" became an ideological shorthand for cultural work in the nineties, it was a vision struggling to be born in the gravitational field of the storytelling festival lineup. The schedule in 1985, for instance, included Spalding Gray, the autobiographical monologuist from New York City; traditional musician/storytellers from Ethiopia (Selashe Damessae) and Bengal (Purna Das Baul); a professor, Robert Creed, whose specialty was reciting Beowulf in Old English; a 78-year-old retired children's librarian, Alice Kane, born in Belfast and raised in Toronto; a Pueblo Indian novelist and poet, Simon Ortiz; Mary Carter Smith, a self-styled African-American "Urban Griot" from Baltimore; Penninah Schram, from New York, who specialized in Jewish folktales; a teacher from St. Louis, Lynn Rubright, who had developed large-scale pilot programs for storytelling in schools; Connie Martin, a colleague of Robert Bly in the use of folktales as heuristic tools in revisioning gender roles; revival performers with backgrounds in writing (Jay O'Callahan), theater (Jon Spelman), mime (Jackson Gillman), and music and dance (Heather Forest); and the great traditional Jack tale teller Ray Hicks. "These performers represent a wide range of styles and stories, traditions and cultures," wrote festival director Laura Simms in the program guide. "In 13 years, NAPPS has successfully created a place for storytelling as an important social, political, and healing art."

What Simms meant by linking those three dimensions—social, political, and healing—in her mission statement, has to do with Robert Cantwell's interpretation of festival magic. The careful calibration of cultural representation in the construction of the festival program became for her and others a potent metaphor for the ritual construction of a peaceable kingdom. Geographic, ethnic, racial, gender, and stylistic balance are not casual matters in this construction, but matters of world-shaping import.

On Saturday, the formal storytelling activities run from 10 in the morning until 10:30 at night, in all the tents and the Swappin' Ground. Each featured performer generally has one one-hour slot to him- or herself, then two or three other sessions that are shared with one to three other tellers. Sometimes these group sessions are planned around a theme—in 1985, themes included "Men's Stories," "Women's Stories," "Stories of the West," "Heroes," "Laughing Stories," "Stories With Music," "True Stories," and "Family Stories"—sometimes the theme is only implicit in the contrasting voices of the tellers. Inevitably, one is drawn and quartered by one's appetite for things going on in many separate sites, until one is forced to surrender to the narrowness of a personal agenda. Apprentice storytellers and fans pick a favorite, or two, three, or four favorites, and try to follow them from tent to tent, studying and enjoying them under different conditions, large tent and small, alone and in various combinations, watching them work off of one another and off of the energy of different crowds. It is an opportunity to be imprinted, as a teller, by stories and by telling styles that resonate particularly with one's own personality and background—that reach inside and awaken some slumbering sense of personal voice and vocation.

By late Saturday afternoon, the vision (or more precisely, the audition) of revived tradition, or of a polyphony of revived traditions all caroling their anthems under the banner of NAPPS, has been largely set in place, and the place prepared for the arrival and assumption of Ray Hicks. The staff car pulls up to the Tent in the Park, covered with dust from the mountain roads. The designated driver gets out to help Hicks unfurl his astonishingly elongated frame. His wife Rosa, tiny and thin as a six-penny nail, follows him out carrying bags of ginseng, sassafras, and angelica root gathered from the mountain, and some homemade apple cakes, all for sale. Whether Hicks is late for his show or not, he is instantly surrounded.

Children and adults, friends, acquaintances and strangers, storytellers and tourists stop to ask him questions, to listen to his torrent of talk, to snap his picture, or just to gawk. Hicks's image has adorned so many posters, flyers, schedules, programs, not to mention newspaper and magazine articles on the festival over the course of 20 years, that it seems for a moment as if the festival itself has stepped out of a car and stands waving its enormous arms between the resource tent and the road.

This synecdoche remains compelling despite the fact that no one could be less typical of the contemporary storyteller bred by the revival and the festival than Hicks. Though the festival would move more and more towards professional tellers who were quite at home in the segmented world of the weekend schedule, it still needed as its symbol a man whose stories and whose entire consciousness came self-evidently from outside that world, and were only subject to being contained within it for brief, ritual descents, one Saturday afternoon a year. The Christian ritual, by analogy, takes as its centerpiece a man who was both born in a manger and immaculately conceived. The incarnation of American storytelling in a cabin on Beech Mountain that has neither heat, running water, television, nor clocks is a similar boon to the devout imagination.

In McConnell's unofficial Friday appearances he would act as a forerunner to Hicks's storytelling messiah, baptizing visitors in Appalachian storytelling traditions in preparation for Hicks's Saturday descent from the Mountain of Transfiguration. The difference in their repertoires is appropriate to this complementarity. Tall tales are worldly and rough; Jack tales, for all Hicks's characteristic interruptions, are most often otherworldly, supernatural, and associated with the Jungian archetype of the sacred child. Tall tales play with exoteric/esoteric code-switching. Hicks's long wonder tales, particularly in his archaic dialect, are purely esoteric, difficult to listen to, but rewarding the faithful with microcosmic epiphanies of the total storytelling revival myth.

After Hicks and his wife have been bundled into the car and driven away back up the mountain, there is a break for dinner. Food courts line the parking lot between the big Tent in the Park and the smaller tent on the hill. The resource shed, later to grow into a tent of its own, is open and booming; all the restaurants in town are full. These free, informal zones in the tightly scheduled weekend are the times when the web of personal connections are formed which will give a sense over the course of the year and the years that there is such a thing as a national storytelling community. Relationships are deepened—sometimes with acquaintances from home who suddenly become, in this weightless sphere, the people in the world who most closely share your soul; sometimes with strangers from half a continent away who catch your eye and wind up sitting across from you in a heart-to-heart outpouring all the more passionate the further it soars from your daily life—all this in the altered, festival state of emotional susceptibility brought on by two days on a constant roller coaster of narrative movement.

After dinner there is another scheduled session, a kind of mini-olio, in which two to five tellers play off of one another in each of two to five tents. The sun has set. Stories told can deepen and darken, revealing new comic, tragic, or personal dimensions. There is a sense of immanence, of a premonitory excitement leading up to the ghost story session. The accumulated invocations of ancestors, of otherworldly visions, and of hostile, benevolent, or tutelary spirits thicken the atmosphere of dusk.

Until 1985, all other activities would stop at 9 p.m. and crowds would gather at the foot of the hill northeast of Main Street for the walk to the cemetery for the ghost telling. The seasonal approach of the old Celtic New Year, the divide between the light and dark halves of the year, when the gates between the worlds stand open for a night, adds an atavistic shiver to the natural chill in the air. In the ritual form of the festival, this is the traditional descent into the Underworld, with the storytellers as shamanic guides. It is an opportunity to contemplate the lower, malevolent, and fearsome forms on the other side of the divide of life and death.

In the mythos of the storytelling revival, the ghost telling has a dual resonance. In addition to being inevitably the most popular and profitable event of a storytelling festival, ghost storytelling is one of the last living refuges for traditional oral narrative in contemporary American popular culture. Whether on Boy Scout trips, at summer camps, or on junior-high-school sleep overs, there remains a lively tradition of keeping the darkness homeopathically at bay with hoary old legends and gruesome new inventions. So as midnight approaches, the ritual dramatization of the revival myth deepens, in a thicket of subliminal paradox. Through the imagining of death—our own as shivering mortals, paired with the projected death of storytelling as an art form and divine scapegoat–audience and art form are titillated into a state of exaltation. Though pronounced dead and buried over and over, here is the art of storytelling risen before us, reminding us that we are alive by leading us to the brink of annihilation—to sites in the imagination where resurrection of the body is worse than death. "Go back to the grave," cries the father in "The Monkey's Paw," refusing the temptation to wish his dead son back in the flesh. While Jackie Torrence was telling this story in the cemetery in 1985, a drunken fan went wild, shouting, "Jackie, Jackie, I love you, Jackie!" with such mournful exuberance that she fell off the porch of the decrepit old house where she was standing, and had to be carried away. It was the last ghost telling in the Jonesborough cemetery, and a chilling glimpse of what it might be like to have the art of storytelling resurrected in the hungry flesh of American celebrity-worship.

After midnight, the crowd is released. It streams down the hill like a fleet of candles in the dark, burning with the light of an art which has just been struck to life. After a short night of dreams, the festival faithful resurrect into the light of the sacred telling. These two events, ghost telling and sacred telling, are twinned in the ritual structure of the festival, dark giving way to light, yang to yin. The stories told here all concentrate on positive images of spiritual experience. Revenants appear only to wipe a weeping eye and tell their loved ones they are at peace. Wailing and gnashing of teeth are stilled by a kind word or a gentle touch, from this world or the next. Gods and goddesses, saints and bodhisattvas play peekaboo from behind the fleshly masks that show to the world as bag ladies or simpletons. The holy fool sleeps forever in the divine mother's arms, and the sibilant whisper of palm rubbing palm would not disturb his sleep.

At the height of the revival period, the sacred telling was the climax of the festival for festival initiates, as the ghost storytelling was its climax for the merely curious. Many of those who streamed down the hill from the cemetery would not come back, but would go away satisfied with the metaphysical teasing of the ghost stories. Those who were waiting to find a redemptive vision in storytelling would return in the morning for the sacred telling. The spiritual worlds depicted on Saturday night were exciting precisely because they were sundered from this world by great gulfs of fear. The spiritual worlds depicted on Sunday morning were gently joined to this one by currents of love, mercy, forgiveness, and courage.

Like many another liminal rite, the trajectory of the festival moves downward into the dark in order to push the spirit up into the light. The revival preacher takes care to draw his eager audience into the steaming pit of hell before raising them into the dawn of salvation. The tribal initiate may be symbolically buried or dismembered before being reincorporated into his new status. At the storytelling revival event, once again, the symbolic protagonist of festival's ritual narrative is storytelling itself. Featured tellers and committed audience celebrate the sacrificial death of the folk art, its harrowing of the hell of our haunted imaginations, and its resurrection as a tool of social connectedness and spiritual healing. By our projected identification with and dedication to the storytelling form, we are moved to shed fears and doubts and take on some of the power demonstrated at the festival, for reincorporation into our own lives and home communities.

WORKS CITED

Campbell, Joseph. *The Hero with a Thousand Faces.* Princeton: Princeton UP, 1972.
Martin, Rafe. Telephone interview. 21 Jan. 1992.
May, Jim. Telephone interview. 16 Apr. 1992.
McConnell, Ernest "Doc." "Tucker's Knob." *Storytelling: The National Festival.* Audiotape. Jonesborough: NAPPS, 1983.

Propp, Vladimir. *Morphology of the Folktale.* 2nd ed. Austin: U of Texas P, 1968.
Shannon, George. "Dear Yarnspinner." *Yarnspinner* 6.12 (1982): 1-3.
Simms, Laura. "Welcome to the National Storytelling Festival." Festival brochure. Jonesborough, TN: NAPPS, 1985.
Torrence, Jackie. Telephone interview. 23 Jan. 1992.
Turner, Victor. *The Ritual Process.* Ithaca: Cornell, 1979.
Van Gennep, Arnold. *The Rites of Passage.* Trans. by Monika. B. Vizedome and Gabrielle L. Caffee. London: Routledge and Kegan Paul, 1977.

WORKS CONSULTED

Birch, Carol. Telephone interview. 10 Apr. 1992.
Cantwell, Robert. "Conjuring Culture: Ideology and Magic in the Festival of American Folklife." *Journal of American Folklore* 104.412 (1991): 148-63.
—. "Response to Peter Seitel." *Journal of American Folklore* 104.414 (1991): 496-99.
Chase, Richard, ed. *The Jack Tales.* Boston: Houghton, 1943.
Dorst, John D. *The Written Suburb: An American Site, An Ethnographic Dilemma.* Philadelphia: U of Penn, 1989.
Ellis, Elizabeth. Telephone interview. 11 Jan. 1992.
Forest, Heather. Telephone interview. 23 Feb. 1992.
Schechner, Richard. *The Future of Ritual: Writings on Culture and Performance.* London: Routledge, 1993.
Smith, Jimmy Neil, ed. *Homespun: Tales from America's Favorite Storytellers.* NY: Crown, 1988.
Sobol, Joseph Daniel. "Jonesborough Days: The National Storytelling Festival and the Contemporary Storytelling Revival in America." *DAI* 55 (1994): Northwestern U.
Stivender, Ed. Telephone interview. 7 Jan. 1992.
Wallace, Anthony F. C. "Revitalization Movements: Some Theoretical Considerations for Their Comparative Study." *American Anthropologist* 58 (1956): 264-81.

BETSY HEARNE
Associate Professor
Graduate School of Library and Information Science
University of Illinois at Urbana-Champaign

Midwife, Witch, and Woman-Child: Metaphor for a Matriarchal Profession

My great-grandmother had a passion for healing. Although she never gave and received pills or injections of any kind, she delivered babies and cured or eased both herself and many others through time-tested herbal recipes meticulously written out in a Swiss-German Amish dialect. When she cut her hand open with a butcher knife, she sewed it back up again with a boiled darning needle. She was still canning and baking her own bread at the age of 94. After her husband of 30 years died, she sat up all night with his body, as was the custom. Sometime toward morning, according to my mother, she left her rocking chair and walked slowly to the coffin. Then she began to probe, from head to toe, each part of the man she had loved so long. She stopped at his abdomen, continued, returned to it, probed again, nodded her head, and returned to her chair. He had died of an abdominal tumor that was undoubtedly cancer, and she wanted to know.

My mother told me that story, and this one, too, about the time she went to break up the huge old house filled from cellar to attic with my grandparents'—and great-grandparents'—things. Desperately she discarded, gave away, auctioned, burned, or saved generations of relics. One artifact in question was my great-grandmother's box of herbal recipes. On the phone with my father, she mentioned her quandary over what to do with these recipes. "Throw them away," said my father, the doctor. "They're worthless." I was reminded of this story in reading an account, in Laurel Ulrich's tour de force *A Midwife's Tale*, of how narrowly eighteenth-century midwife Martha Ballard's diary missed destruction:

> When her great-great-granddaughter Mary Hobart inherited it in 1884, it was 'a hopeless pile of loose unconsecutive pages'—but it was all there. The diary had remained in Augusta for more than sixty years, probably in the family of Dolly Lambard, who seems to have assumed custody of her mother's papers along with the rented cow. At Dolly's death in 1861, the diary descended to her

> daughters, Sarah Lambard and Hannah Lambard Walcott. . . . Mary Hobart . . . was thirty-three and a recent graduate of medical school when her great-aunts Sarah and Hannah gave her the diary. "As the writer was a practising physician," she later explained, "it seemed only fitting that the Ballard diary, so crowded with medical interest, should descend to her." (346)

Thus the diary was saved by a hair by an heir, one of the first women doctors in the second half of the nineteenth-century, who commissioned her cousin Lucy to bind it in linen and had a mahogany desk built especially to hold it. Ironically, my father's mother had graduated from medical school at about the same time as Martha Ballard's heir. However, this paternal grandmother died before my mother could ask her the strategic question about the value of herbal recipes.

So it came about that, unlike Martha Ballard's private documents, my great-grandmother's were lost because of my professional father's advice. I have only oral fragments passed on as stories from my mother, and I know that boneset tea, whatever that is, may be one of the few known cures for migraine headache. One other note: in slightly earlier times and places, not only would Great-grandmother Eliza's records have been in doubt, but also her life. While obstetrics has not generally been considered a dangerous occupation, midwifery sometimes was. The designations of healer, midwife, and witch overlapped precariously, depending on patriarchal authorities and public mood. French historian Jules Michelet, in a classic nineteenth-century study recently re-published as *Witchcraft, Sorcery, and Superstition,* elaborates on what happened when the midwife-healer was labeled "witch" for applying her skills:

> The Sorceress was running a terrible risk. Nobody at that time had a suspicion that, applied externally or taken in very small doses, poisons are remedies. All the plants which were confounded together under the name of *Witches' herbs* were supposed ministers of death. Found in a woman's hands, they would have led to her being adjudged a poisoner or fabricator of accursed spells. A blind mob, as cruel as it was timid, might any morning stone her to death, or force her to undergo the ordeal by water or *noyade.* Or, worst and most dreadful fate of all, they might drag her with ropes to the church square, where the clergy would make a pious festival of it, and edify the people by burning her at the stake. (83)

Of course, male doctors used some of the same plants; midwifery and the medical profession had much to learn from each other (as did—loath though clergymen might have been to admit it—witchcraft and church doctrine). However, women in creative touch with nature were in danger of being seen as supernatural rather than natural. "Nature makes them sorceresses," quotes Michelet in reflecting the sixteenth-century attitude toward women associated with pantheism (*viii*). Giving birth and delivering life were too powerfully mysterious not to be threatening. Where there's life, there's death only a fragile breath away; and women who controlled life might also have controlled death. Writes Ulrich about Martha Ballard's patients, "Between 1767 and 1779, Oxford lost 12 percent of its population in one of the worst diphtheria epidemics in New England's history. One hundred forty-four persons died, mostly children ages two to fourteen" (12). And this was not even a plague era. In one year, Martha lost three of her nine children, her uncle and aunt, eight of their eleven children, friends and neighbors, and many more. Fortunately, no finger of suspicion was ever pointed at Martha, as we shall consider later, but in face of uncontrollable, mysterious, threatening forces there often lurked the question: Who more than the life-bringer could be blamed for bringing death?

And what does all this have to do with children's literature? Be patient. Perhaps a storytelling link is already apparent. The midwife/witch/healer turns out to be a common archetype in children's literature, a genre midwifed and nurtured by women. From a historical perspective, the parallels between midwives delivering babies, midwives delivering nascent children's literature, and midwives appearing as characters in children's literature may come as no surprise.

Martha Ballard learned some of what she knew from her own Grandmother Learned, still alive in 1777, the year before Martha delivered her first baby (Ulrich 11-12). Wise Child, in Monica Furlong's juvenile novel of that title, learns herbal lore from midwife/witch/healer Juniper, who learned it from midwife/witch/healer Euny. Brat, a.k.a. Alyce in the Newbery Award book *The Midwife's Apprentice*, learns what she knows from midwife/healer Jane Sharp. Kit gathers symbolic knowledge from elderly Hannah in Elizabeth Speare's *The Witch of Blackbird Pond*: "Thee did well, child, to come to the Meadow. There is always a cure here when the heart is troubled" (85). Humpy, a.k.a. Lovel in *The Witch's Brat* by Rosemary Sutcliff, learns herbal lore from his healer/witch grandmother, though he does not have her Second Sight. Rosemary in *Becoming Rosemary* absorbs the gift of healing from her midwife/witch/healer mother. Ugly One in *The Magic Circle* first learns the trade of herbal lore from her healer/witch mother:

> She pointed out the herbs. She showed me the medicinal value of the hare's liver. She revealed to me the secrets of the river fish. I know cures from her. And through the years I have added my own. I have experimented, always following my instinct. But until now my cures have been offered only to newborns and their mothers and to my own sweet Asa. My heart is now in my throat. My breath comes hard. "I would heal if I could." "Then we must make you a magic circle," says Bala. "You can stay entirely within the magic circle, and no devil can get you." (Napoli 12)

Like Ugly One, Laura Chant—heroine of Margaret Mahy's *The Changeover*—crosses the line from natural to supernatural in trying to heal her brother, and she does it, like Wise Child and Euny, under the supervision of two older women who have done it before her. Say Laura's mentors, "We will marry you, if we can, to some sleeping aspect of yourself and you must wake it. Your journey is inward, but it will seem outward" (139). In each of the seven children's books mentioned, we see a knowledge of special power developed within a matriarchal network for passing on that knowledge.

Among the several patterns immediately apparent in children's fiction about midwife, witch, and woman-child, then, is the intimate passage of intimate lore from masters to apprentices. The master is a mature or elderly woman, the apprentice a prepubescent girl (with the exception of one boy marginalized by his crippled body), and both are typically different from others, often community outcasts or at best tenuously accepted if and when the regnant patriarchal society requires their skills. The apprenticeship is difficult, demanding, and ultimately dangerous because the female healer is dealing in the art of life and death. Her observations of nature involve a closeness to nature that is suspect in the eyes of the church and other male-dominated institutions. Women's sexuality is suspect because it is associated with the inevitable but mysterious power of birth and death, with the rhythm of moon and tides so often metaphorical of female cycles as to become a romanticized stereotype. (Less than romantic is the solution of Meghan Collins' "The Green Woman" to hedge her bets on herbal remedy by sending her own virile lover to bed the governor's wife, who has threatened to foment a witch trial unless the Green Woman can guarantee her an infant heir to the governor.)

THE MIND-BODY CONNECTION

The art of healing, as all of these apprentices learn, has to do with mind as well as body. Learning, as implied by the status of apprenticeship itself, has to do—amazingly enough—with education. Mental and spiritual health is crucial to physical health. And what, it turns out, is more crucial to spiritual health than storytelling and, even more specifically in each of these books, reading? "Juniper told me some amazing stories," says Wise Child in detailing her education in Celtic lore and later in literature. "I wanted to learn, too, to lose myself in the pleasure of books, of stories and thoughts . . ." (Furlong 178). Kit, who teaches children to read through storytelling in *The Witch of Blackbird Pond*, passes on her old silver filigree hornbook to a child as isolated as herself (Speare 105). The shy orphan Alyce learns to read from a scholar who pretends to be teaching the cat: "Once Alyce knew all the letters and a number of combinations, Magister Reese began teaching the cat words, reading aloud bits of wisdom from his great encyclopaedia" (Cushman 79). Ugly One has learned to read from the father of her illegitimate child and uses a local burgermeister's books to study the skills and sorcery of healing. Lovel learns to read at the monastery from an illustrated book of physic herbs, "And all the while, though he was not properly aware of it, the old wisdom and the old skills that were in him from his grandmother were waking more and more; the green fingers that could coax a plant to flourish and give its best; the queer power of the hands on sick or hurt bodies (Sutcliffe 38).... He seemed to be seeing with his hands as well as feeling" (40).

Not only are storytelling and reading crucial in all of these books, but there is also a persistent association of storytelling and reading with magic. Indeed, Rosemary's strangely powerful older sister Con reads her mother Althea's books from a distance; the family knows because they see the pages turning by themselves while Con is minding pigs in the forest.

> Althea owned three books, books that Rosemary's grandmother had owned, and her great-grandmother before that.... Sometimes Rosemary would be alone in the house, and she would walk by the table to see that one of the books had been pulled away from the others and opened. Slowly, very slowly, the pages would turn, as if blown by a breath from far away.... Sometimes, when Rosemary saw those pages turning, she would run into the forest so that she could find Con and sit and listen. (Wood 49-50)

Magic associated with storytelling and reading may symbolize the more mysterious, intuitive, associative, or subconscious aspects of learning. We are to some extent moved and transformed by stories in inexplicable ways that seem to involve a metaphorical process important to understanding the human condition. Inherent in the work of healing is passing on knowledge not only of the ingredients, but of how and in what circumstances they are effective, how people respond to them in unexpected ways, how people react to life and death. This kind of knowledge is wisdom—not information. It has to do with instinct, experience, observation, and values, as well as facts. What each apprentice learns from her mentor comprises much more than plant names and applications. Despite our scientific era, we still speak of the "art" of healing. Each of the apprentices must learn to honor her creative self, nurture her full identity, and pass on her knowledge in an oral or printed tradition before becoming a master of her art.

Like the Fates who determine life and death on spindle or loom, these women often practice—in addition to the art of healing—the art of spinning and weaving. It's a domestic art, of course, but with a mythological resonance that's closely associated with the art of spinning a yarn, the art of storytelling. And the stories of these women, when they reach us, make gripping literature as well as historical lore. Here is a dramatic example linking the long, tedious birth attendances in the almost-lost diary of Martha Ballard, a weaver of flax, by the way, and a spinner of wool (we'll come back again later to women's proclivity for applied arts, generally underrated in comparison to "fine arts"). This entry is from April 24, 1789:

> A sever Storm of rain. I was Calld at 1 hour pm from Mrs Husseys by Ebenzer Hewin. Crosst the river in their Boat. A great sea A going. We got save over then sett out for Mr Hewins. I Crost a stream on the way on fleeting Loggs & got safe over. Wonder full is the Goodness of providence. I then proceeded on my journey. Went beyond Mr Hainses & a Larg tree blew up by the roots before me which Caused my hors to spring back & my life was spared. Great & marvillous are thy sparing mercies O God. I was assisted over the fallen tree by Mr Hains. Went on. Soon Came to a stream. The Bridg was gone. Mr Hewin took the rains waded thro & led the horse. Asisted by the same allmighty power I got safe thro & arivd unhurt. Mrs Hewins safe delivd at 10 h Evn of a Daughter. (Ulrich 6)

Ulrich astutely points out the rhythm, repetition, and pattern of alternating "action sentences with formulaic religious phrases" here (7). It seems clear that in another age, Ballard might have been a noted writer as well as a noted physician. We must ask ourselves if what she was, a great midwife and storyteller, is any less for having been unnoted.

Martha Ballard, without her 27-year diary, would have been recorded in public documents no more than the three times a woman was supposed to be for birth, marriage, and death (Tucker 8). Says Ulrich,

> The American Advocate for June 9, 1812, summed up her life in one sentence: "Died in Augusta, Mrs. Martha, consort of Mr. Ephraim Ballard, aged 77 years." Without the diary we would know nothing of her life after the last of her children was born, nothing of the 816 deliveries she performed between 1785 and 1812. We would not even be certain she had been a midwife. (5)

The only testimony we have of Ballard's service and talents is a private record, which Ulrich has proven accurate through painstaking cross-checks with public records, available from the same time period, of environmental disasters such as flooding or of religious/political upheavals to which Ballard refers tangentially. Knowledge in the form of history, literature, arts, and sciences has traditionally been divided into public and private domains, the public belonging to men and the private to women, the former considered, until recently, to be of greater significance than the latter (Welter).

Moving Beyond the Household Stage

More specifically, Western (and many non-Western) cultures have divided storytelling into public and private domains, with men in charge of the public and women of the private. Audiences for men tended to be other men in context of religious rituals or political arenas while audiences for women tended to be children and other women, on a household stage. Extreme examples of this division, in current or recent practice but rooted in ancient rites, are the exclusion of women from the Hassidic storytelling tradition and, indeed, the exclusion of all Orthodox

Jewish women from the synagogue room where readings of the Torah take place during Sabbath services; the prohibition against women's performing publicly in fundamentalist Islam; the prevention of women from administering priestly rites and sermons in the Catholic church; and the definition of pre-World War II East European coffee houses as a platform for male epic singers (see Lord's *The Singer of Tales*). All the cultures involved here have a strong female storytelling tradition, but it is confined to the private domain. Parallels can be seen in the history of art, in which men have been more commonly acknowledged for painting and other "formal" graphic media, while women have only recently been counted artists for their work on quilts, knitting, sewing, embroidery, rugs, pottery, etc., all family-centered activities with practical applications. An interesting philosophical question might revolve around whether a lullabye sung through thousands of nights is of equal value to a symphony written by one whom the lullabye shaped.

In the folkloristic realm, Charles Perrault, Jakob and Wilhelm Grimm, Andrew Lang, and Walt Disney all took stories collected primarily from women in domestic situations and translated them onto a public academic and/or commercial stage. This translation legitimized what had earlier been held in low esteem as old wives' tales. Even the fairy tales published by women such as Charlotte-Rose de Caumont De La Force, Marie-Jeanne L'Héritier, and Marie-Catherine D'Aulnoy never achieved the status of work by intellectuals such as Perrault, the Grimms, and Lang, who had broader literary or nationalistic agendas.

During the late nineteenth and early twentieth centuries, especially in Britain and the United States, women began to make a transition from storytelling in the private domain to storytelling in the public arena. With increasing access to education, they started to publish fiction—cf. Nathaniel Hawthorne's letter to his publisher: "America is now wholly given over to a damned mob of scribbling women and I should have no chance of success while the public taste is occupied with their trash and should be ashamed if I did succeed " (Wagenknecht 150)—but much of their work took the form of short stories in magazines for women and children, as opposed to "serious fiction," an area still dominated by men at that time (Shaker 6-7). Similarly, the rise of professionalism among women saw them going primarily into service professions that represented an extension of domestic duties: nursing (taking care of children's bodies) and social work, teaching, or librarianship (taking care of children's minds and spirits). As women pushed into the world of publishing, they were most frequently allowed toeholds in a relatively new business: translating an old literature for children, often folklore passed on by women, into a new literature for children, also cultivated by women (Hearne, "Margaret K. McElderry" 755-775).

Children's book publishing became a women's world that continued the old domestic gender patterns in a public arena, though it was a public arena significantly less valued than that of adult literature. With very few exceptions, women produced the books, edited the books, purchased the books, and inducted younger women in the ongoing cycle. As authors, editors, publishers, and librarians, women formed a flexible network with much role-switching between creative and administrative functions, just as women's creations have often blended art and application. Perhaps it is not surprising, then, that studies show girls as more avid readers, especially of fiction. They are part of a gender-shaped storytelling tradition that is even now extending the oral/print transition into electronic media. In their role as tradition bearers in both oral and print modes, women have midwifed children's literature, and children's literature about midwife/witches—all by women—reflects a reverence for tradition so pronounced that it's open to parody by scholars such as Diane Purkiss, who questions contemporary revisions:

> Although we no longer fear the witch, we still have not owned those dark feelings. Rather, we have sanitised the witch, so that she can become acceptable, transforming her into another one of our better selves. Now she is clean, pretty, an herbalist with a promising career in midwifery, a feminist, as good a mother as anybody if not rather better than most, sexually liberated (without being too kinky). (282)

It is important to stress that the old girls' network, as idealized as it may be in the old girls' literature—see, for example, quotes in Vandergrift (706) and Bush (732)—is no more ideal than the old boys' network. Where there are issues of power, there are always related issues of control that can be exaggerated, in fact, if the power is seen as scarce or limited within a broader social context. Children's literature—attended by matriarchal midwives who are neither perfect nor perfectly compassionate, but powerful in their own sphere (as we see in Cushman's portrayal of Jane Sharp and Mahy's of Miryam and Winter Carlisle)—recreates the stereotype of good and evil witches by idealizing the former while the latter, only by implication, lurk unacknowledged somewhere in the shadows. Ironically, today's literary witch believes, as did some seventeenth-century witches, in her own magical powers despite the intervening period when educated feminists saw witches as victims innocent of anything more powerful than superstitious and homicidal public opinion. The midwife/witch's magic currently represented in children's fiction is, like the seventeenth-century witch's magic, both powerful and threatened, both devoted to traditional female values and subversive of patriarchal values.

Midwife/witches and their apprentices in juvenile fiction are a paradox of tradition and subversion. They follow the hero-journey cycle: cast out from society; summoned by destiny to travel through temptations and tests, often in the company of an animal helper; surviving the rite of passage to return to society or create a new one based on newly acquired knowledge. How old can this story pattern be? The knowledge of these women, and their stories, is subversive in viewpoint only; the narrative structure is as conservative as possible. It's what they do and tell, not how they do or tell it, that breaks boundaries. Folklore is often subversive in content, rarely in form, and these women are traditional storytellers, tradition bearers.

THE TRADITIONAL BECOMES SUBVERSIVE

Children's literature is, in fact, often radical in subject but conservative in style. I have dealt at length with this idea elsewhere in examining both formally conservative children's fiction such as Penelope Lively's (Hearne, "Across the Ages") and folkloric form in popular picture books (Hearne, "Perennial Picture Books"), but the point has a place here in relation to the academy that today privileges us to evaluate storytelling and criticize children's literature. Having touched on parallels of midwife/witch in history and midwife/witch in children's literature, I want to touch on midwife/witch in the library profession and its academic training grounds where, to some extent, the traditional has again become subversive.

Like midwives, weavers, and storytellers, the women who delivered children's literature and librarianship did not separate theory from practice or art from application. Moreover, the scholarship of Jane Anne Hannigan, Kay Vandergrift, Christine Jenkins, and Anne Lundin, among others, shows over and again how deeply this women's field has depended on longterm anonymous service, flexible role changing, cooperative networking, mentoring relationships, nonconfrontational resistance, and low-profile leadership. These are not characteristics highly rewarded in contemporary academia despite lip service to several of them. As the Dean of the Social Sciences at the University of Chicago said recently, in closing down the School of Education (five years after the closure of the university's Graduate Library School), "we can't let a sentimental concern for children get in the way of hard scrutiny about whether we are producing quality work" (Bronner A27).

Just as children's literature was the female domain of a male-dominated publishing world, the critical evaluation of children's literature was fostered by female-dominated children's specialists in libraries and library education for nearly a century before entering the minds or departments of male-dominated English Literature and Education departments in the 1970s. That entry, signaled by the involvement of male critics, has changed the critical evaluation of children's literature, and we need to think about how and why in determining a new balance of scholarship. Escalating attempts to make children's literature competitively prestigious with adult literature have resulted in some prose as impenetrable as the briars surrounding Sleeping Beauty, an apt comparison considering that only a select prince could find his way through. In a recent *Horn Book Magazine* article, "How to Get Your Ph.D. in Children's Literature," Brian Alderson points to the absurdity of a critical stance and language that feeds on itself instead of on literature. Perpetrating a classic hoax, he submitted a proposal to analyze *The English Boy's Magazine* to conference organizers who described it as excellent and enthusiastically invited him to present the paper.

> My starting point will be an attempt to rescue the concept of *parole* from that of *langue*, perceiving a need for saussurian theoretics to give way in the analysis of socially designed texts to the more flexible critical potential residing in the insights of Bakhtin and Althusser. I will develop this through an examination of the dialogic qualities in the Empire-building serials by H.P Anelay, discussing not merely the nature of the intentionality of these essentially propagandist works but also the nexus of authorial discourse and readerly expectation.... I would assess the connotative semiotics of the printed image. This may lead me towards the unexplored territory of pictorial content as subliminal discourse in this instance on the hegemony of the imperial ethic. (439)

Alas, confesses Alderson, "there was no such thing as an *English Boy's Magazine* published from 1886 to 1902, nor any such person writing serials under the name of H.P. Anelay, nor any illustrator of those serials signing W.B.," as a check of any "shelf of mundane reference books on children's literature" (440) would have shown. What Alderson's hoax shows up is a concern more for academic status than for children's literature.

In its struggle for validation in a male-dominated hierarchy, is the literary criticism of children's books "growing up" to fit male-defined requirements? (Obviously, critics of both genders vary individually. I am looking not at individuals but at gender patterns—as in noting, for example, that not all men have been U.S. presidents but all U.S. presidents have been men.) At a recent international conference on children's literature, all four plenary session speakers were men, this despite the overwhelming majority of female presenters and attendees, not to mention the singular domination of women in the history of children's literature.

WOMEN'S QUIET SUSTENANCE

To some extent, the same pattern exists in the field of fairy tales, folk tales, and storytelling. Perhaps the most famous men to put fairy tales on the modern academic map have been Bruno Bettelheim, who championed them upon a towering theoretical superstructure of Freudian interpretation, and Jack Zipes who challenged him with a Marxist reading. Relatively unnoticed has been the quiet, consistent women's work, especially in the field of librarianship, that sustained the study and practice of folk and fairy tales in children's culture for a hundred years prior to Bettelheim's recommendations in *The Uses of Enchantment.*

Marie Shedlock, Ruth Sawyer, Sara Cone Bryant, Gudrun Thorne-Thompsen, Anna Cogswell Tyler, Mary Gould Davis, Eileen Colwell, Ruth Tooze, Augusta Baker, and many others spent their professional and intellectual lives advocating—and acting on—the delivery of folk and fairy tales to children. In his book *Creative Storytelling,* Zipes describes storytellers who visit schools and libraries. More often, however, school and public librarians *are* storytellers dedicated to just the kind of community-building he advocates, and an integral part of that community, as well. If their work has not been theoretically subversive, the very act of their sustaining storytelling programs decade after decade in the face of budget cuts and skeptical authorities *has* been subversive, not to mention the fact that Molly Whuppie and other active folktale heroines were mainstays of such programs from the turn of the century, long before politically corrected anthologies began to surface in the 1970s. Zipes himself is a strong feminist, but many folklorists, perhaps politically sensitive to their own insecure academic status, have consistently distanced themselves from the female- and child-associated areas of storytelling in librarianship and children's literature (Hearne, *Beauty* 148-154). Where is the story of the storytellers, the women who turned school boiler rooms and store fronts into houses of story in both oral and print traditions?

School and public librarians share stories with children on a weekly basis without seeking either stardom or fancy fees. They have been doing it for a hundred years. Yet one male scholar at the aforementioned international conference publicly praised another male scholar for the singular feat of going into schools and working with children himself. The parallel might be Columbus discovering America. Could such disregard for indigenous inhabitants be due to an undervaluing of female librarians' and library educators' traditional treatment of literature as an applied art? Has their work been at once discounted and coopted? Or has it simply been unnoted?

While some fairy tale scholars—a few female, but more often male—have become academic supernovas, the women who kept folklore, fairy tales, and juvenile literature alive in libraries and library education for a century have faded from graduate school curricula (see Lundin's survey results in "The Pedagogical Context of Women in Children's Services and Literature Scholarship"). An escalating academic struggle for resources, time, and attention endangers awareness of the kind of invisible presence and quiet voice on which service-oriented women in children's literature and librarianship have typically relied to get their work done. The words "web" and "webbing" appeared frequently (even before web-*masters* commandeered the World Wide Web) in describing women who led the field of children's literature/librarianship—and spiders, though effective, are notably silent. It is time to project our voices beyond the professional web, to define ourselves to a broader public community as women have done in other disciplines.

Psychologist Carol Gilligan talks about the way females characteristically develop a sense of justice as compromise rather than contest, an "ethic of care" (171-74). Anthropologist Nancy Chodorow describes women's blurred sense of ego boundaries as a basis for empathy. Philosopher Elizabeth Minnich asks us to create gender-inclusive curricula "recovering women's stories within the complex intellectual traditions of higher education" (Lundin 841). Sociologist Harriet Presser explains how, for many academic women, the personal is political *and* professional in *Gender and the Academic Experience* (141-156). What are the implications, for specialists in children's literature and librarianship, of these and many other voices examining intellectual midwives past and present?

As a public-domain institution the university is still close to patriarchal conventions. Remember that only in the past 50 years have women worked their way toward becoming a substantial percentage of faculty and heads of universities (the latter still deeply under-represented). And only in the last 25 years have women worked their way toward becoming subjects of history, literature, and science curricula in mainstream institutions. Women's stories, women's studies, women's development, it's still relatively new stuff—new enough to be considered trendy and token rather than deeply imbedded and distributed. It's subversive stuff, and few claim to know exactly what it is or where it belongs. Often women's studies units run the risk of becoming marginalized. Isolated midwives, as we know from the history of witch-hunting, were in a dangerous position. Alas, Wise Child and Juniper had to be rescued by Juniper's ex-true-love playing deus ex machina with his sailing vessel anchored just out of reach of a pursuing mob—a 1987 resolution remarkably parallel with that of the 1958 book, *The Witch of Blackbird Pond*, 30 years earlier.

The most successful midwives—in terms of not getting burned at the stake—were those imbedded deeply within the community rather than marginalized on its fringes. Nobody bothered historical midwife Martha Ballard in the 27 years of her midwifery, and nobody bothered literary midwives Althea in *Becoming Rosemary* or Jane Sharpton in *The Midwife's Apprentice*. These three characters, one actual and two fictional, were careful to remain encompassed in community. Indeed, community was the strength of successful midwifery. Historically, as many as four to six women, with tasks requiring varied levels of skill, attended a birth under the direction of a midwife.

By the same token, children's literature and librarianship cannot afford to be isolated from mainstream academia, including the information science component of LIS, the theory-driven bastions of postmodern English departments, and the education schools that are pushed to embrace quantifiable test-score approaches to learning. And yet children's literature/librarianship must also work to define, maintain, and assert its valuably distinctive—and distinctively female—balance between the creative and analytic, practical and theoretical, private and public, personal and objective, artistic and scientific, traditional and innovative.

As a survivor of conflicts between these forces, which are so often divided in educational institutions—the "higher" the education the more polar the division—I nurture stories. My job is to tell stories about stories, to help deliver other people's stories, to examine stories, to keep the process healthy. Relevant to my understanding of this process is having birthed stories myself. Ulrich quotes an eighteenth-century midwifery manual to the same effect, that having babies was part of the preparation for delivering them (12). (This, needless to say, might not have proved popular with male doctors as a standard requirement.)

The story, its procreation; the literature, its practice: these are integrated, interactive processes. Let's not throw away the box of recipes. Although still suspect (for example, see Ritter's newspaper reports, "Midwives Battle State Crackdown" and "A Tough State for Midwives"), midwifery is in many circles increasingly valued as an integrated, interactive way to deliver babies. And it is no accident that metaphors of midwifery fit smoothly in a matriarchal profession that has delivered the private domain of storytelling into the public domain of children's literature.

WORKS CITED

Alderson, Brian. "How to Get Your Ph.D. in Children's Literature." *The Horn Book Magazine* 73 (1997): 437-441.
Bettelheim, Bruno. *The Uses of Enchantment: The Meaning and Importance of Fairy Tales.* New York: Vintage, 1977.
Bronner, Ethan. "End of Chicago's Education School Stirs Debate." *The New York Times* 17 Sept. 1997: A27.
Bush, Margaret. "New England Book Women: Their Increasing Influence." *Library Trends* 44 (1996): 719-735.
Chodorow, Nancy. "Family Structure and Feminine Personality." *Woman, Culture, and Society.* Eds. Michelle Zimbalist Rosaldo and Louise Lamphere. Stanford: Stanford UP, 1974. 43-66.
Collins, Meghan B. "The Green Woman." *Don't Bet On the Prince: Contemporary Feminist Fairy Tales in North America and England.* Ed. Jack Zipes. New York: Methuen, 1986.
Cushman, Karen. *The Midwife's Apprentice.* New York: Clarion Books, 1995.
Furlong, Monica. *Wise Child.* New York: Knopf, 1987.
Gilligan, Carol. *In a Different Voice.* Cambridge: Harvard U P, 1982.
Hearne, Betsy. "Across the Ages: Penelope Lively's Fiction for Children and Adults." *The Lion and the Unicorn,* in press.
—. *Beauty and the Beast: Visions and Revisions of an Old Tale.* Chicago: U of Chicago P, 1989
—. "Margaret K. McElderry and the Professional Matriarchy of Children's Books." *Library Trends* 44 (1996): 755-775.
—. "Perennial Picture Books: Seeded by the Oral Tradition." *Journal of Youth Services,* in press.
Lord, Albert B. *The Singer of Tales.* Cambridge: Harvard U P, 1960.

Lundin, Anne. "The Pedagogial Context of Women in Children's Services and Literature Scholarship." *Library Trends* 44 (1996): 840-50b.
Mahy, Margaret. *The Changeover: A Supernatural Romance.* New York: Atheneum/Margaret K. McElderry, 1984.
Michelet, Jean. *Witchcraft, Sorcery, and Superstition.* Prev. pub. as *Satanism and Witchcraft.* New York: Carol, 1995.
Napoli, Donna Jo. *The Magic Circle.* New York: Dutton, 1993.
Presser, Harriet. "The Personal is Political *and* Professional." *Gender and the Academic Experience.* Eds. Kathryn P. Meadow Orlans and Ruth A. Wallace. Lincoln: U of Nebraska P, 1975. 141-56.
Purkiss, Diane. *The Witch in History: Early Modern and Twentieth-Century Representations.* London: Routledge, 1996.
Ritter, Jim. "Midwives Battle State Crackdown." *Chicago Sun-Times* 11 Sept. 1997: 3.
—. "A Tough State for Midwives." *Chicago Sun-Times* 15 Sept. 1997: 6.
Shaker, Bonnie James. "Kate Chopin and the Birth of Young Adult Fiction." Address. History of Print Culture Conference. Madison, Wisconsin, 9 May 1997.
Speare, Elizabeth George. *The Witch of Blackbird Pond.* Boston: Houghton, 1958.
Sutcliff, Rosemary. *The Witch's Brat.* London: Oxford U P, 1970.
Tucker, Susan. "Reading and Re-reading: The Scrapbooks of Girls Growing Into Women, 1880-1930." Address. History of Print Culture Conference. Madison, Wisconsin, 9 May 1997.
Ulrich, Laurel Thatcher. *A Midwife's Tale: The Life of Martha Ballard, Based on her Diary, 1785-1812.* New York: Knopf, 1990.
Vandergrift, Kay E. "Female Advocacy and Harmonious Voices: A History of Public Library Services and Publishing for Children in the United States." *Library Trends* 44 (1996): 683-718.
Wagenknecht, Edward. *Nathaniel Hawthorne: Man and Writer.* New York: Oxford UP, 1961.
Welter, Barbara. "The Cult of True Womanhood, 1820-1860," *American Quarterly* 18 (1966): 151-74.
Wood, Frances M. *Becoming Rosemary.* New York: Delacorte, 1997.
Yolen, Jane. *Here There Be Witches.* San Diego: Harcourt Brace, 1995.
Zipes, Jack. *Creative Storytelling: Building Community, Changing Lives.* New York: Routledge, 1995.

Works Consulted

Bateson, Mary Catherine. *Composing a Life.* New York: The Atlantic Monthly Press, 1989.
Arbuthnot, May Hill. *Children and Books.* Chicago: Scott Foresman, 1947. (See also 2nd-4th editions under Arbuthnot and 5th-9th eds. under Sutherland, Zena.)
Baker, Augusta and Ellin Greene. *Storytelling: Art and Technique.* New York: Bowker, 1977.
Bauer, Caroline Feller. *Handbook for Storytellers.* Chicago: American Library Association, 1977.
Baxandall, Rosalyn and Linda Gordon, eds. *America's Working Women: A Documentary History, 1600 to the Present.* Rev. ed. New York: Norton, 1995.
Brink, André. "The Writer as Witch." *The Dissident Word: The Oxford Amnesty Lectures 1995.* Ed. Chris Miller. New York: Basic Books, 1996. 41-59.
Colum, Padraic. *Story-Telling, New and Old.* 1927. New York: Macmillan, 1968.
Colwell, Eileen, ed. *A Storyteller's Choice: A Selection of Stories, with Notes on how to Tell Them.* New York: Walck, 1964.
Conway, Jill. *True North: A Memoir.* New York: Knopf, 1994.
Cook, Elizabeth. *The Ordinary and the Fabulous: An Introduction to Myths, Legends and Fairy Tales for Teachers and Storytellers.* 2nd ed. Cambridge: Cambridge U P, 1976.
Ehrenreich, Barbara and Deirdre English. *Witches, Midwives and Nurses: A History of Women Healers.* Old Westbury: Feminist Press, 1973.
Ellis, Sarah. "Pinch." *Back of Beyond: Stories of the Supernatural.* New York: Simon Schuster/Margaret K. McElderry, 1997.
Forbes, Thomas Rogers. *The Midwife and the Witch.* New Haven: Yale U P, 1966.
Franklin, Penelope, ed. *Private Pages: Diaries of American Women 1830s-1970s.* New York: Ballantine, 1986.

Hannigan, Jane Anne. "A Feminist Analysis of the Voices for Advocacy in Young Adult Services." *Library Trends* 44 (1996): 851-874.
Heilbrun, Carolyn G. *Writing a Woman's Life.* New York: Norton, 1988.
Jenkins, Christine. "Women of ALA Youth Services and Professional Jurisdiction: Of Nightingales, Newberies, Realism, and the Right Books, 1937-1945." *Library Trends* 44 (1996): 813-39.
Johnson, Edna and Carrie E. Scott, eds. *Anthology of Children's Literature.* Boston: Houghton, 1935. (See also later editions in 1940, 1948, 1959.)
Linde, Charlotte. *Life Stories: The Creation of Coherence.* New York: Oxford U P, 1993.
Lively, Penelope. *Oleander, Jacaranda: A Childhood Perceived: A Memoir.* New York: Harper, 1994.
Monter, E. William. "The Pedestal and the Stake: Courtly Love and Witchcraft." *Becoming Visible: Women in European History.* Ed. Renate Bridenthal and Claudia Koonz. Boston: Houghton, 1977.
Orlans, Kathryn P. Meadow and Ruth A. Wallace, eds. *Gender and the Academic Experience: Berkeley Women Sociologists.* Lincoln: U of Nebraska P, 1994.
Paley, Vivien. *The Boy Who Would Be a Helicopter: The Uses of Storytelling in the Classroom.* Cambridge: Harvard U P, 1990.
Pellowski, Anne. *The World of Storytelling.* New York: Bowker, 1977.
Pierson, Kate. "Knocking Down Straw Women: Re-examining the Premises of Feminist Folklore Anthologists." Masters thesis, U of Chicago, 1989.
Poovey, Mary. *The Proper Lady and the Woman Writer: Ideology as Style in the Works of Mary Wollstonecraft, Mary Shelley, and Jane Austen.* Chicago: U of Chicago P, 1984.
Rich, Adrienne. *Of Woman Born: Motherhood As Experience and Institution.* New York: Norton, 1976.
Rosaldo, Michelle Zimbalist and Louise Lamphere. *Woman, Culture, and Society.* Stanford: Stanford U P, 1974.
Sawyer, Ruth. *The Way of the Storyteller.* New York: Viking, 1942.
Schimmel, Nancy. *Just Enough to Make a Story: A Sourcebook for Storytelling.* 3rd. ed. Berkeley: Sister's Choice Press, 1992.
Shedlock, Marie L. *The Art of the Story-Teller.* 1915. Rev. ed. New York: Dover, 1951.
Smith, Karen, ed. "Imagination and Scholarship: The Contributions of Women to American Youth Services and Literature." *Library Trends* 44 (1996).
Steedman, Carolyn Kay. *Landscape for a Good Woman: A Story of Two Lives.* New Brunswick: Rutgers U P, 1987.
Stephens, John. "Witch-figures in Recent Children's Fiction: The Subaltern and the Subversive." Address. International Research Society of Children's Literature. York, England, 26 Aug. 1997.
Stewig, John Warren. "The Witch Woman: A Recurring Motif in Recent Fantasy Writing for Young Readers." *Children's Literature in Education* 26 (1995): 119-33.
Walsh, Elsa. *Divided Lives: The Public and Private Struggles of Three American Women.* New York: Anchor-Doubleday, 1996.
Webber, Jeanette and Joan Grumman, eds. *Woman As Writer.* Boston: Houghton, 1978.
Zipes, Jack. *Breaking the Magic Spell: Radical Theories of Folk and Fairy Tales.* New York: Methuen, 1984.
—. "Tales Worth Telling: Searching for Stories that Challenge Our Poisonous Myths." *Utne Reader* (September/October 1997): 38-42.

MALORE I. BROWN
Assistant Professor
School of Library and Information Science
University of Wisconsin-Milwaukee

Evaluating Stories for Diverse Audiences

> Legends take us back to the origins of the tribal people, to their hopes, struggles and defeats. There are many cultures which have stories that are not readily available in print. The information is not found in libraries, but exists within the hearts and minds of individuals called Storytellers.
>
> Legends are a celebration of the human spirit, part of our American tradition, and the history of our country. To this very day they are being told, altered, and retold. In this book, the author attempts to present an interesting version of chanted literature. The legends are told in his voice, echoing the voices of his ancestors. The author does not attempt to present the only account or version of the legend, nor does he wish to offend similar tribal Storytellers. If the reader enjoys these myths, the author in retelling them has achieved his purpose.
>
> It is important to understand the roles and power of the Storyteller. These oral historians are given the responsibility of remembering and reciting their Native American Culture. It is through their ability that we understand their true heritage. (Cuevas 2)

I would like to share an example of evaluating stories for diverse audiences with a diverse group. At the University of Wisconsin-Milwaukee School of Library and Information Science, I teach a class called "Multicultural Literature for Children and Young Adults." This past spring, I had a very diverse group of students registered in the course. The group included two African-American females in their late 20s, one African-American female in her early 40s, one Caucasian female in her mid-40s, several Caucasian females in their mid-30s, one African-American male in his mid-30s, and one Caucasian male in his early 30s. I started the semester with the basic lecture about what to look for when evaluating materials—plot, theme, style, etc. By the second or third class session we were evaluating books. I had the idea of evaluating that very old story, Helen Bannerman's *The Story of Little Black Sambo,* which had been reissued in two different versions in 1996: Julius Lester's *Sam and the Tigers*, illustrated by Jerry Pinkney, and Bannerman's *The Story of Little Babaji*, illustrated by Fred Marcellino. Each student read the new editions and was required to go to the university library and look at two of the older editions, with Bannerman's original text, in the historical collection.

I have a rule in my classes when we discuss and evaluate materials: we mention the good qualities of the item first and the negative last. This is to ensure that the students do not get drawn into a purely negative discussion and never get around to the positive attributes of a work.

I opened the discussion of these three books by asking for reactions and thoughts from class members. One of the twentysomething African-American females said she had never seen *The Story of Little Black Sambo* and she was glad to be able to look at it, but she "didn't know what all the fuss was about." She also thought the illustrations—which have caused a great deal of controversy—were funny. The discussion took off from there! The fortysomething African-American woman explained the hurt and hatred those illustrations caused during the racial turmoil of the 1960s. The fortysomething Caucasian woman said she had received an original copy of *The Story of Little Black Sambo* as a child and had hated the illustrations but loved the story. The discussion moved to *Sam and the Tigers*, which includes a source note from Lester about *The Story of Little Black Sambo*. Some of the students loved *Sam and the Tigers*, and others hated it. One of the stated reasons for disliking the book was the fact that all the characters were named Sam. Everyone loved the Bannerman book (illustrated by Marcellino), *The Story of Little Babaji*, except for the African-American male, who suggested that the illustrations stereotyped Asian Indians. And the discussion continued. This was an example of evaluating a story and two variants of that story. Evaluating stories in print is a challenging task and even more challenging with a diverse group.

The issues are similar in storytelling. These students of different races, sexes, and ages had very different reactions to the story variants they studied, reactions that depended on their cultural experiences as well as their individual viewpoints. So, too, will a storytelling audience bring their own cultural perspectives to the story they hear. The creators of these variants were also responding, consciously or unconsciously, to cultural contexts for *The Story of Little Black Sambo;* so, too, must storytellers engage with the cultural contexts of the stories they tell.

The Importance of Research

The most common obstacle to the powerful telling of a story is the teller's lack of knowledge; research into the background of tales can allow the storyteller to enhance and add credibility to already powerful storytelling. The teller is encouraged to use indexes and collections to research variants and origins, to enhance the story development and enrich the telling. Aarne and Thompson's *The Types of the Folktale,* Eastman's or Ireland's *Index to Fairy Tales,* and Margaret Read MacDonald's *The Storytellers Sourcebook* offer a starting point. Other worthwhile resources available for teller research include motif indexes, examinations of folk culture, dissertations on folklore, discussions of superstition and the supernatural, dictionaries of folk language and expressions, encyclopedias of folklore, collections of stories, riddles, rhymes, and jokes, and the list goes on. Story collections themselves often provide substantial background, since some print variants include a source note to assist in the understanding of a story. Betsy Hearne, in her July 1993 *School Library Journal* article "Cite the Source: Reducing Cultural Chaos in Picture Books, Part One," proposed that producers of picture-book folktales provide source notes that set these stories in their cultural context and that those of us who select these materials for children consider how well the authors and publishers meet this responsibility in our evaluation of such books.

Using the indexes, poring through collections, and finding source notes is time consuming, so why should a teller go through all of this work? Because knowing more about the history and origin of a tale allows the storyteller to immerse him- or herself in the story and understand it better, thereby telling a believable story and increasing his/her level of comfort in the retelling. The research conducted by a storyteller often reveals overlooked or hidden qualities of a story and allows the teller to relate that story with greater detail and knowledge, becoming a clearer vehicle. The more the teller is able to learn about the many elements of a particular story, the truer the voice of the story will be (Livo and Rietz 10). A serious storyteller will eventually need to look beyond the text of the story to learn to tell the story well; an informed storyteller enhances the story and renders a rooted and credible telling. Acknowledging the sources, whether the story is documented in folklore, heard from another person, or read somewhere, sets the story in context and allows listeners to prepare themselves accordingly. As a storyteller becomes familiar with the culture of a story, a sense of confidence, authority, and authenticity begins to emerge.

There are many forces at work in the making of a story. Knowing the requirements, conventions, and etiquettes of the culture generating a tale pulls the storyteller closer to it. The actual creativity of the teller adds to these forces. Without adequate background on the contents of a story, the teller may not be able to convey the story's themes or know what kind of creative latitude, linguistic and otherwise, is appropriate. Oftentimes, for instance, stories make references to artifacts (Pellowski 216). Usually the artifacts are not incidental or utilitarian. They carry special cultural meaning important for understanding the stories. For example, if a story makes use of a mango tree from which the protagonist picks a fruit, meanings indigenous to a specific culture and the hidden implications of the reference are important. Substituting a more contemporary or local, more recognizable tree may violate the integrity and meaning of the story.

African stories are often characterized by a particular kind of oral tradition. Many of the stories are "pourquoi" or "why" stories," stories which explain animal and human characteristics. The repetitive language and styles that encourage interaction with the storyteller make them excellent choices for sharing but also reflect a particular cultural tradition. Personified animals, often tricksters, are popular subjects for African folktales as well as folktales of other cultures.

Many North American folktales and stories have roots in the cultures of other parts of the world or have been influenced by written literature. Identifying tales that began in a specifically North American oral tradition may be difficult or impossible. Four types of folktales found in North America have been identified by researchers: Native American tales that were handed down over centuries of tribal storytelling; folktales that came from African countries and were changed over time, becoming African-American tales; European tales containing traditional themes, motifs, and characters that were changed to meet the needs of the New World; and boastful tall tales that originated on this continent.

Native American tales are usually considered the only traditional tales truly indigenous to the United States. Some Native American tales have motifs in common, but differ in other ways from region to region and tribe to tribe. Many of these are, like African stories, pourquoi tales, explaining why or how animals obtained specific characteristics. Like people in many other cultures, Native North Americans also have mythology that explain the origins of the universe and natural phenomena. Magical animal trickster figures such as Rabbit, Coyote, or Raven are also popular in Native American culture. In addition, traditional tales of legendary heroes reflect many important values and beliefs of various groups. These legendary heroes have many of the same qualities found in heroic tales from other cultures.

Maintaining a balance between story traditions and invention during the story delivery is the responsibility of the storyteller; it always has been. The teller who becomes a student of a story's folkloric substance can better balance story form and invention, and can support a more powerful delivery. To tell a story well, with power and with honesty, one must know more than just the story, and one must achieve a necessary intimacy with its "life world" (Livo and Rietz 2).

EVALUATION OF STORIES

Before discussing the selection of stories for a diverse audience, it is important to discuss the selection and evaluation process of stories in general. Researchers stress a holistic approach to the evaluation of stories prior to telling, emphasizing the necessity of examining theme, characterization, setting, and style. These are important elements in the success of a good tale no matter what audience the tale is for. Most important in evaluating and selecting stories for a diverse audience is to use the same critical guidelines that are used in selecting mainstream materials. In evaluating stories, tellers must first ask if the tale is well written or translated. Equally important are the setting and point of view. The setting of the story should be clear, believable, and authentic. The details should be natural and interwoven into the action. Just as in mainstream stories, characters should be believable and have depth. Interactions between the characters should sound natural and unforced. The story should hold the attention of the listeners within a credible sequence of events. Tales should succeed in arousing the interest of the listener and the teller. In essence, the selection process for stories of diverse cultures does not differ greatly from the selection and evaluation process of mainstream stories. We still look for cultural accuracy to insure that issues are represented in ways that reflect the values and beliefs of that culture.

Stories from all cultures portray the struggles, feelings, and aspirations of common people; stories depict the lives of the rich and poor; and stories reflect the moral values, social customs, superstitions, and humor of the times and societies in which they originated. There are stories from every culture that include appreciation for the beauty and mystery of life and belief in the power of the spirit to accomplish its will. Some stories are comedic, others tragic, but all reveal the depth of human values. Anything is possible in stories as long as it is faithful to the truths of the heart.

STORIES AND AUDIENCES

If a teller tells tales from cultures that have a particular connection to a specific audience, listeners will come to the tales with certain expectations and perhaps even a sense of possession, which the teller needs to honor. I grew up in an extended family. When my mother and father were married, my father had five children living with him ranging from an eight-year-old to several teenagers—all his nieces and nephews. It was a time when many Jamaicans went abroad, either to England or the United States, in search of work. Once they got established, they would send for their families. My mother entered into the relationship with two younger sisters and a grandmother, my great-grandmother. Everyone affectionately called my great grandmother "Granny." Granny was old from the day I was born, bless her soul, and she died at the ripe age of 92 in 1980. Granny was a storyteller. She told Anancy stories. I never knew how she came up with so many Anancy stories. These trickster tales always held our attention. Imagine my surprise when, many years later, my mother and I were at the Milwaukee Public Library's used book shop and there was a book of Anancy stories; from Africa, no less! I was in high school at the time. I said to my mother, "I thought those were Granny's stories! Someone stole her stories and published them." And then my mother explained that Granny had heard them from her mother, who was a slave, and those stories were brought from Africa. These stories were both part of the culture of African storytelling and part of my culture as a listener to the point where I was shocked to see those tales outside of my family; the Anancy stories are so much "Granny's stories" to me that I still can't bring myself to tell them.

Yet many tales and their cultural origins will be new and different to some audiences. Traditional folk literature, tales originally handed down through centuries of oral storytelling, offers an opportunity for an introduction to another culture in the form of stories that many listeners will enjoy. New listeners gain a respect for the creativity of the people who originated the stories, develop an understanding of the values of the originators, and share enjoyable experiences that have entertained others in centuries past.

We analyze folklore to make discoveries about the types of stories represented, as well as the cultural patterns, values, and beliefs reflected in tales. The teller and listener may notice how many values and beliefs are common to many cultures: the importance of maintaining friendship, a need for family loyalty, the desirability of genuine hospitality, the use of trickery, gratitude for help rendered, respect for courage, and awe of the supernatural. Storytellers are conservators of the memories of oral cultures. Knowing cultural significance and symbolic contents of artifacts can aid the teller in telling and imparting meaning.

Research and background work help establish standards for selecting and evaluating stories for diverse audiences. The identification of high-quality stories helps to bring together the teller and the listener, in addition to instilling in both a deeper understanding and appreciation for the tale's culture of origin.

By studying a culture, we can discover which aspects of its stories are indeed part of the life of that group, and we can also select other culturally relevant details to add to our retellings (Sierra and Kaminski viii). As we enjoy another culture's stories, we extend our knowledge of and sensitivity to the global community.

Editor's Note: An additional annotated listing of Brown's reference tools is included in the appendix of this volume.

Works Cited

Aarne, Antti. *The Types of the Folktale: A Classification and Bibliography*. 2nd rev. Trans. Stith Thompson. Helsinki: Academia Scientarum Fennica, 1961.
Bannerman, Helen. *The Story of Little Babaji*. New York: HarperCollins, 1996.
—. *The Story of Little Black Sambo*. London: Grant Richards, 1899.

Brown, Malore Ingrid. *Multicultural Youth Materials Selection.* Diss. U of Wisconsin, Milwaukee, 1996. Ann Arbor, Mich: UMI, 1997. 9715455.

Cuevas, Lou. *In the Valley of the Ancients: A Book of Native American Legends.* Albuquerque: Petroglyph National Monument, 1996.

Eastman, Mary Huse. *Index to Fairy Tales, Myths, and Legends.* 2nd ed. Boston: Faxon, 1926.

Hearne, Betsy. "Cite the Source: Reducing Cultural Chaos in Picture Books, Part One." *School Library Journal* 39 (1993): 22-27.

Ireland, Norma Olin. *Index to Fairy Tales 1949-1972.* Westwood: Faxon, 1973.

Lester, Julius. *Sam and the Tigers: A New Telling of Little Black Sambo.* New York: Dial Books for Young Readers, 1996.

Livo, Norma J. and Sandra A. Rietz. *Storytelling Folklore Sourcebook.* Englewood: Libraries Unlimited, 1991.

MacDonald, Margaret Read. *The Storyteller's Sourcebook: A Subject, Title, and Motif Index to Folklore Collections for Children.* Detroit: Neal-Schuman/Gale Research, 1982.

Pellowski, Anne. *The World Of Storytelling.* Bronx: Wilson, 1990.

Sierra, Judy and Robert Kaminski. *Multicultural Folktales: Stories to Tell Young Children.* Phoenix: Oryx Press, 1991.

WORKS CONSULTED

Baker, Augusta and Ellin Greene. *Storytelling: Art and Technique.* 2nd ed. New York: Bowker, 1987.

Bauer, Caroline Feller. *Caroline Feller Bauer's New Handbook for Storytellers: With Stories, Poems, Magic, and More.* Chicago: American Library Association, 1993.

Caduto, Michael J. and Joseph Bruchac. *Keepers of the Earth: Native American Stories and Environmental Activities for Children.* Golden: Fulcrum, 1988.

MacDonald, Margaret Read. *The Storyteller's Start-up Book: Finding, Learning, Performing, and Using Folktales Including Twelve Tellable Tales.* Little Rock: August House, 1993.

Once Upon A Folktale: Capturing The Folklore Process With Children. Ed. Gloria T. Blatt. New York: Teachers College Press, 1993.

Ross, Ramon Royal. *Storyteller.* 2d ed. Columbus: Merrill, 1980.

Shedlock, Marie. *The Art of the Story Teller.* 3rd ed. New York: Dover, 1951.

Storytelling Concerts

A storytelling conference of course needs storytelling, and the planners of the 39th Allerton Conference made sure it had plenty. At the conclusion of the days' programming on both Sunday and Monday nights, a storytelling concert was held in the library of Allerton House. Conference participants gathered together in the genteel space, encompassed on three sides by vast floor-to-ceiling bookshelves, and on the fourth side by floor-to-ceiling windows.

On Sunday night, Janice Harrington and Dan Keding held the audience with energy and humor. Harrington told traditional folktales, sometimes engaging the audience in boisterous participation. Her awe-inducing delivery of "Tiger's Minister of State," (an African folktale in which Tiger asked each prospective minister if his breath was sweet or sour) had listeners longing for their mouthwash. Keding's Civil War ghost tale about a letter delivered after the death of the writer added a poignant chill to the evening, especially with his a cappella rendition of "Johnny, We Hardly Knew Ye" echoing off the library walls.

For the Monday night concert, Harrington and Keding were joined by the impressive Susan Klein, who told personal tales of growing up on Martha's Vineyard. Keding told stories of his upbringing by his Croatian grandmother on the South Side of Chicago, interspersed with snatches of traditional and original song as he accompanied himself on guitar and banjo. When Harrington wasn't rocking the walls with a mirthful retelling of the African tale "Talk" relocated to the American South, she was wistfully evoking the sorrow of Mother Wind and her lost children. Klein's closing piece was a 30-minute tour de force, an especially moving tribute to a teacher who affected her life forever with his flamboyant flair and love of language. She imitated her erstwhile teacher uttering Keats' phrase "Beauty is truth, truth beauty," in the round, resonant tones of a master of dramatic delivery. The printed page can only hint at the live experience that made the conclusion of each day seem like a new beginning.

JMD

Section Three: Story as Literature

Most of us at the Allerton conference were drawn not just by a love of storytelling, but also by a passion for books, the stories within them, and their relationship to our own stories. Three different speakers focused, in three very different ways, on these literary stories and their connection with the child audience. *Book Links* Editor Judy O'Malley's "Book Linking to Story" examined both the story connection behind many books and the multitude of connections to other stories that a book can provide, showing how a single title can be one crucial link in a chain of story knowledge. In "Narrative in Picture Books," Deborah Stevenson explored the methodology of telling a story in picture book form, discussing the characteristics, advantages, and disadvantages of a story told in two media at the same time. And author-illustrator Arthur Geisert, with his storytelling about his adventures in house building and in storytelling in books, offered a vivid reminder of the relationship between story and biography and the happy result when creativity and craftsmanship give the story a life of its own.

DS

JUDITH O'MALLEY
Editor
Book Links: Connecting Books, Libraries and Classsrooms

Book Linking to Story

We all have stories. For most of us, they start with family stories, oft told and fancifully embroidered. I grew up in a large, loud family where there were stories, but there were also "holes" where stories should have been. Things never talked about, around which stories couldn't grow. It bothered me. There were no stories about my father's side of the family, because some long-ago falling out with his brother closed down all conduits to stories, even the ones from his childhood before the breach. It caused him to devalue the power and need for story. When my father's sister, the only relative we maintained contact with—and only because she wouldn't let us lose the stories—came to visit and shared her lore, my father left the room.

Though my mother always referred to my father's love of history, I rarely saw him read; he often criticized me or my sisters for "wasting time" reading when we could be doing something "useful." The rest of us were and are a family of readers, passing books back and forth, sharing stories from school and bridge club. One person's interest linked to a related book that then dovetailed with another title, seemingly unrelated to the first impulse to "read up." Little did I know that this mesh of oral and written stories was really basic training for my future profession.

There were other kinds of "holes" in the fabric of our stories, too—frayed edges around what were perceived to be our "family matters." That they were not to be shared was implicit, but these memories were frequently off limits for discussion even in the family. Many years later, I understand a bit better. Reading Frank McCourt's *Angela's Ashes*, I started to realize you can't stop story; you can only postpone it for a generation. Then the stories will out, producing not only readers and tellers, but writers, educators, passionate advocates for story. We're all seeking to fill in the holes in our personal and our cultural histories through stories: written stories, told stories, stories in books, movies, even on the Web.

Of course, many of the stories and books I've always gravitated to have centered on the kinds of secrets that so long frustrated me. Secrets within families, governments, cultures, textbook accounts of history; secrets in our own psyches and souls. Whether poetry, mystery, memoir, biography, or autobiography, stories and books usually come down to telling secrets. And children love secrets, for to the youngest the world is full of them. Before adults successfully conspire to turn the thrill of discovery into work, children love to learn because it means deciphering coded messages, knowing the secrets the adults know. Children love to share their secrets, too, to tell the stories they are learning. You can only imagine how much I worried my "keep it close to your chest" parents when I would go visiting in the neighborhood. Like most children, I was a storyteller, and what I knew, I told. Not always appropriate behavior, but very helpful in learning to appreciate and even shape—and surely embellish—a good story.

The need to know and the need to tell drives storytelling, drives learning and fuels understanding. Whether formal or informal, oral or written, stories tell children they are included in the community. Books share with children the rich juicy secrets of life.

Working with articles for *Book Links* often feels like weaving on a loom. A nonfiction book for middle-grade students, *The Dead Sea Scrolls* by Ilene Cooper, the author of many fiction and nonfiction books for children and the Children's Books Editor for *Booklist*, was the focus of a feature article (Cooper, "Dead Sea"). The author describes her fascination with the complex history and significance of the Dead Sea Scrolls. Her desire to tell the story of the scrolls in a way that children could not only understand but find as exciting and intriguing as a mystery or thriller led her to connections with books about archaeology, religion, the history and politics of the Middle East, and even computers, since technology made possible the ultimate reconstruction of the holes in the scrolls' secrets. In the article, Cooper uses the same connecting strands she used in writing *The Dead Sea Scrolls* to link it to books on those subjects for children. When an author shares the threads of facts and ideas that they untangled and wove into a gripping story, children appreciate the texture of that tapestry of story and, hopefully, will be motivated to weave their own stories.

From the earliest years, our lives are filled with story threads. Some of the first stories children learn and hear, the traditional folktales of their particular culture, form the canvas into which other story threads are interwoven. George Shannon shows how one such tale has been the thematic fabric over which other tales have been stitched in an article entitled "The Pied Piper's New Melodies: Folktale Variations." The basic story elements of the Pied Piper have been adapted to suit various genres, settings, social issues, plot twists, and parodies in a range of books, plays, and short stories for adults and young adults, as well as for very young children. The original tale becomes a coded language through which new understanding comes to light. As the article shows, using the "key" of this tale that children know well can be a way to help them appreciate differences in form and structure in various literary genres, in cultural references in other media, and in everyday language. Looking closely at how stories borrow from one another and elaborate on themes builds an appreciation for the ways in which "stories beget stories."

Many of the most ancient myths and folktales were attempts to explain the natural world around us. Children do this instinctively, and we can build on their understandings of the physical world by pairing their observations of science concepts with folktales, picture books, nonfiction, and poetry that explore similar principles from a literary point of view, enriching both experiences. Judy Sima's article, "Story-Enhancing Your Science Lessons," includes suggestions for expanding the impact of science, such as reading Joseph Bruchac's retelling of "Turtle's Race with Bear" in *Iroquois Stories: Heroes and Heroines, Monsters and Magic* to dramatize an experiment with the surface tension of solids and liquid (47). In the story, Turtle wins the race across a frozen pond with the help of relatives who poke their heads up through holes in the ice.

Children do need and want to know about the world, and stories that connect to their lives help them to learn and to care. Eliza Dresang, an associate professor in the School of Information Studies at Florida State University, in her article, "Developing Student Voices on the Internet," explores some of the many Web sites on which children and young adults are speaking out about what matters to them, finding their voices in response to global events and using those true voices to tell their stories. This article connects some of those sites with recent books for young people that also reflect children's voices and experiences. Among the books included are *The Palm of My Heart: Poetry by African American Children*, edited by Davida Adedjouma and gloriously illustrated by Gregory Christie, who received a Coretta Scott King Illustrator Honor Award for this book. That title is an excellent example of how cultural understanding, sharing of secrets, and a foundation for building community can all be fostered through reading, as both the art and poetry of *Palm of My Heart* are imbued with respect—respect for the teller, respect for the listener, respect for the story. A Web site that resonates with this book is *KidsCom*, whose "Make New Friends" page features "graffiti walls" on which kids of various ages can add their thoughts, creating poetry, more story, more secrets to be shared and understood.

Another way to nurture understanding about the world and about shared experiences and different heritages is by giving children access to accurate, realistic stories from and about a variety of cultures other than their own. Consistently encouraging children to read about other cultures helps them to break down artificial barriers and to gain compassion and understanding for all people as individuals, rather than drawing artificial borders between "us" and "others." The International Board on Books for Young People does an inspiring job of turning good books for children into bridges spanning chasms between peoples. "The World of IBBY," by Amy Kellman, provides a list of excellent books for children of all ages that reflect some aspects of the cultures of nations that have IBBY sections.

Linking the stories in books to what children are learning and what they need to know about the world lets the secrets out and turns facts into story—compelling, exciting, living story. Short books of historical fiction for students from kindergarten through the middle grades have the muscle to arouse self-professed nonreaders to the power of story (Sullivan). Some are in picture book format, but with the involving plots and believable characters that older children, as well as young readers, will connect with; others are compact novels that will whet children's appetites for this genre and encourage them to try longer, more intricately plotted works.

Author Deborah Hopkinson, on writing about creating her picture book *Birdie's Lighthouse*, follows the same tack of viewing history as compelling story and offers practical examples of ways to open those stories to children, using every tool at our and their disposal ("Shining Light"). Birdie tells her story through a journal kept during the year her family lives on Turtle Island, where her father, and later Birdie herself, keeps the lighthouse beaming brightly. Hopkinson found books and Internet sites dealing with lighthouses, weather predictions and storms, and journal writing—all important elements in Birdie's story—that teachers and librarians can use to link children to Birdie's experiences and the real period and situation in which they are set.

Bringing stories to children and expanding the story's secret by opening doors to other secrets and new information are what teaching and librarianship are all about. Facts and chronologies begin to make sense, they become something to care about, when readers hear, see, and empathize with human beings much like those who made those events history. Family stories can give new meaning to history and historical fiction can inform family stories. Those oft-heard tales of great-greats echo with new importance when a child reads a gripping story of that ancestor's time and place, whether it is an immigration story or one of wartime life in the States or in Europe.

Books provide connections to distant occurrences, whether those occurrences are distant to readers' physical location or their emotional space; connections through books allow readers to empathize with characters, to superimpose human faces and feelings onto events that may be outside their personal experiences. These bridges of books act as links between the author and the reader, characters and the reader, ideas and the reader. The power of these links, and our commitment to making them, cannot be overestimated.

Works Cited

Adedjouma, Davida. *The Palm of My Heart: Poetry by African American Children.* New York: Lee & Low, 1996.

Bruchac, Joseph. "Turtle's Race with Bear." *Iroquois Stories: Heroes and Heroines, Monsters and Magic.* Trumansburg: Crossing Press, 1985. 51-53.

Cooper, Ilene. "The Dead Sea Scrolls." *Book Links* 6 (May 1997): 16-20.

—. *The Dead Sea Scrolls.* New York: Morrow Junior Books, 1997.

Dresang, Eliza T. "Developing Student Voices on the Internet." *Book Links* 7 (Sept. 1997): 10-15.

Hopkinson, Deborah. *Birdie's Lighthouse.* New York: Atheneum Books for Young Readers, 1997.

—. "Shining Light on History." *Book Links* 7 (Nov. 1997): 35-40.

Kellman, Amy. "The World of IBBY." *Book Links* 7 (Sept. 1997): 31-34.

KidsCom. "Make New Friends." 16 June 1998. <http://www.kidscom.com/orakc/Friends/newfriends.html>.

McCourt, Frank. *Angela's Ashes.* New York: Scribner, 1996.

Shannon, George. "The Pied Piper's New Melodies: Folktale Variations." *Book Links* 7 (Sept. 1997): 36-39.

Sima, Judy. "Story-Enhancing Your Science Lessons." *Book Links* 7 (Jan. 1998): 46-53.

Sullivan, Kathleen. "Short Historical Fiction to Get Children Reading." *Book Links* 7 (Nov. 1997): 58-63.

DEBORAH STEVENSON
Associate Editor
The Bulletin of the Center for Children's Books
Graduate School of Library and Information Science
University of Illinois at Urbana-Champaign

Narrative in Picture Books or, The Paper That Should Have Had Slides

I'm not sure my title is quite right—while the product is a unified one, I think there are narra*tives* in a picture book, not just one narrative. As Perry Nodelman says:

> [the picture book] is unique in its use of different forms of expression that convey different sorts of information to form a whole different from the component parts—but without those parts ever actually blending into one, as seems to happen in other mixed-media forms such as film and theater, so that someone reading a picture book must always be conscious of the differences of the different sorts of information. (21)

The literary world is so verbally attuned that it's easy to consider narrative as words only, and therefore to consider a picture book as a narrative with pictures; the art world focuses on the pictures, considering the picture book as an art object with extended captions. These views both seem to me unfortunately limited—if narrative were merely the words on a page, people wouldn't attend conferences—and this side-taking also seems to me to overlook the nature of the picture book as synthesis of art and words. To read a picture book aloud, as most were intended, is to dramatize it. One might almost consider a picture book a variant of a play, one that carries its own set design with it.

In this sense picture books resemble other combinative art forms, such as opera or musical theater, films, and ballet; older examples include the courtly masque and the emblem book. This resemblance is good for me, since I thrive on analogies (I was apparently permanently warped by that section of the SATs), and I therefore often find it useful to consider picture books along with those other media, without, of course, ignoring the fact that picture books also have their own individual charms and characteristics. I'd like to examine the aspects of the picture book—the text, the art and other physical factors—and then discuss how these narratives work together to affect each other and the final outcome.

TEXT: THE DOWNTRODDEN PARTNER

Despite its primacy, the text is often the downtrodden partner in the picture book form. A picture book can, after all, be a picture book without a text; it can't be one without pictures. It's tempting to consider the relative responses to the term "textbook" and the term "picture book"; the former is dull, the term occasionally used pejoratively; the latter is pleasurable and imaginative. Because the text of a picture book is short (*Where the Wild Things Are* by Maurice Sendak contains 338 words in all), the writing of it can seem easy; because the text accompanies pictures, it may seem insignificant. This apparent insignificance can lead to underestimation of the author's role. It's difficult, for instance, for the author of picture books to gain a reputation solely for that skill; many of the best known write for older readers or illustrate as well. The number of critical articles addressing picture book illustration far outweighs those dealing with picture book text, nor is it usual for the author of a picture book to win any writing award such as the Newbery (Nancy Willard's medal for *A Visit to William Blake's Inn* is an obvious exception, but one that was supported by well-received illustrations that made the title a Caldecott Honor book as well). The late Margaret Wise Brown was one of the first picture book authors to gain wide repute; two of the currently most prominent are Eric Kimmel and Robert San Souci, both of whom specialize in folktale adaptation, a type of text that frequently draws more attention, because of cultural interests, than does an original story (Tony Johnston is one of the writers of original texts whose reputation is growing). A likelier way to gain an authorial reputation is as a part of an author-illustrator team, such as Arthur Yorinks and Richard Egielski or Jon Scieszka with Lane Smith (Scieszka's one book with a different illustrator was nowhere near as successful); better still, create both text and art and allow the illustrator's fame to be the same as the author's.

This deceptive simplicity of picture book texts may be one reason why it's so easy to find bad ones. It can become a vicious and self-fulfilling circle: since it seems so easy to write a picture book, it must mean that anyone can, and picture book texts are further cheapened. Picture book authors are also likelier than illustrators to think or be told to think in terms of education rather than art. The pressure on a picture book to be educational, whether pedagogically, politically, or socially, falls almost entirely on the text, so desirable subject matter or an important message can outrank good writing. I have no objection to narratives with lessons: most stories have a point, and didactic tales are alive and well and often absorbing and frequently well-received by children as well as adults, but a lesson in itself is not sufficient for a story. Some picture books seem quite content with the idea that pictures exist as sugarcoating for the textual pill, because that arrangement relieves the text of the burden of being interesting;

the result is artistically inferior and unappealing to most children and adults.

Fortunately, however, many writers of picture books craft their work well, rising to the challenge of writing a text that will meet an illustrator at least halfway. The restraint involved in writing a picture book is a challenge; authors of other kinds of books generally employ narrative to tell the "whole" story, but picture book text must leave some meaning to the illustrations while still possessing its own spirit. It is the text through which adults hope to shape children and inspire them, and the text that an adult will reread a multiplicity of times to an importunate child.

The reading aloud is an important consideration, since most literary texts are designed with a different kind of reading experience in mind. It's odd that the otherwise perceptive Nodelman, in his *Words About Pictures*, a detailed examination of the operation and process of picture books, focuses almost entirely on silent reading of the written text; he finally suggests that the "ironies and rhythms" he analyzes may not be apparent if those texts are read aloud (263). In practice, this seems incorrect. Most picture book creators seem attuned to the auditory aspects, since with most picture books those ironies and rhythms are generally most apparent when the book is read aloud as intended. Many picture book texts read quite blandly on the page, but their patterns of rhythm and energy appear with force when one speaks them aloud.

There are a multiplicity of possibilities even in this compressed and focused genre that will change the narrative completely: the text prose or rhymed; present tense or past; first person, second person, or third person. From a formal point of view, a text can be visually end-stopped, to borrow a term from poetry, with sentences completed before every page turn, or there may be visual enjambment, with sentences continuing through page turns, as in *Where the Wild Things Are* when Max makes "mischief of one kind// and another." The text may be separated from the art (as in *Wild Things*), interspersed with it, or winding around it; or it may only appear in speech balloons (Raymond Briggs' *Father Christmas*). Every page may have text, or text and illustration pages may alternate; or illustration alone may carry many spreads (*Wild Things* again). Or it might be primarily a wordless book with only a small bit of text (Rathmann's *Good Night, Gorilla*). Even before you get to the myriad vagaries of individual style, there are narrative choices that will change a story completely.

As there are, of course, with the illustrations.

The Language of Illustrations

I've found it very challenging, at times, to write about picture books, because the critical vocabulary is geared to words. The term "text" in critical circles, meaning the thing that is contained within every edition of the book, that sense of a title that exists without regard to the physical objects, linguistically excludes illustration. In a larger sense, however, picture book illustration is inarguably part of (and in wordless books, completely) a picture book's text; it is read, it conveys intentional and unintentional meanings, it imparts the story.

As someone whose skills lie entirely in the writing area of the equation, I find myself overwhelmed with the technical side of illustration, with gouache versus watercolor, with color separations each painted in black and then photographed in a different color, with selecting two different kinds of black inks to approximate the brown tones on an original (as happened for Tom Feelings' *The Middle Passage*). I find it hard to imagine making it beyond these technicalities to the creative sweep of artwork, but I suppose it's not that dissimilar to fierce preferences for certain wordprocessing software, an understanding of the different effects between the passive and active voice, or the authenticity conferred by specificity.

Yet every technical aspect of illustration is an aspect of the visual narrative. Oils tell a story differently from watercolor, photo collage from pastels. Black and white (Isadora's *Ben's Trumpet*) obviously differs from color (Ehlert's *Circus*), or even from sepia tones or other monochromatic palettes (Van Allsburg's *The Sweetest Fig*) and even other black and white (Van Allsburg's *Jumanji*); illustrators, like filmmakers, know that the pictorial narrative changes if the colors are different. Look, for instance, at the stylistic and color differences between wordless books, which remove the additional possibility of textual difference (*Anno's Journey* and Raymond Briggs' *The Snowman*).

Differences in the visual treatment make for a completely different narrative. Sometimes it's a matter of interpretation. We're all familiar with songs that have been covered by two different artists. The difference can be substantial (I'm particularly remembering the anecdote about music-hall legend Marie Lloyd performing a rendition of the innocent drawing-room song "Come into the Garden, Maud" that had critics of her morality blushing on account of what they allowed into their own homes). That additional effect can be entirely the province of illustration. It's impossible that a story would be the same when illustrated by David Wisniewski as by Chris Van Allsburg, or by Ed Young and by Arthur Geisert.

Even very small differences alter the construction of the visual narrative. Betsy Hearne has a nifty set of slides that she uses in teaching—the artist Adrienne Adams redid her pictures for Priscilla and Otto Friedrich's *The Easter Bunny That Overslept* 20 years later, and the two sets of illustrations make a provocative contrast. The artist has clearly gained in skill and expertise over the years, and the changes are in keeping with the enhanced sophistication and subtlety of the genre and printing technology; the later illustrations have subtler hues compared to the primary colors of the earlier versions, and the compositions have gotten more diverse and less uninflected, and there's much more sensitivity to the sweep and drama of line. The text remains the same and the pictures are really only slightly altered. Yet, the result is not the same story.

There is always the question of the necessity of such artistic achievement when the young audience may well not notice. I go now for my analogy to the world of musicals for Oscar Hammerstein's metaphor—he pointed out that when the Statue of Liberty was carved, Bartholdi took pains with the top of her head even though he had no reason to believe anyone was going to see it. Merit lies in careful craftsmanship of areas that few will notice as well as those that all will notice; Hammerstein was discussing underlying musical themes and verbal plays that may not be noticed as they go by quickly in live theatre, but are nonetheless there.

And, of course, people do now see the top of the Statue of Liberty's head. Changing times mean different viewpoints and different sets of knowledge, and contemporary children are much more visually schooled than previous generations. Take, for example, the Cottingley fairy incident, which is depicted in a movie called *Fairy Tale* in the U.S. For those who don't know the incident, a pair of young sisters, at the beginning of the century, claimed that fairies were visiting their garden and that those visitors had been captured on film—and indeed, they had pictures of themselves with fairies so convincing that Arthur Conan Doyle, for instance, believed them. Yet these photographs very obviously, to modern eyes, feature living girls and cardboard cutout fairies. Even without tackling the issue of our greater skepticism about such visitation, our visual sophistication makes differentiating between cardboard cutouts and real figures elementary . . . my dear Watson.

Visuals, after all, have their own language; some of it is literal, but some of it, particularly in narrative, is not. Apparently, for instance, many small children have difficulty understanding the convention that sequential pictures of the same object indicate the passage of time rather than just several similar objects at the same time. It's also possible that a child who has recently learned that the shimmers of green and yellow outside do constitute a tree will not be overjoyed at an Impressionist's careful return to the predistinguished vision. Nor is it fair to judge children's visual sophistication by their capability in production. Adults, after all, do not necessarily appreciate a mediocre violinist just because they are themselves execrable musicians. Evelyn Goldsmith notes the difficulty children have in recognizing some theoretically "childlike" abstractions (150). What we have here is a literary and artistic equivalent of what psychology terms the "fis phenomenon," wherein a child whose developing motor skills aren't yet up to the consonantal cluster pronounces "fish" "fis," but whose linguistic knowledge makes him insist that an adult's use of "fis" was incorrect; his ability to produce lags behind his ability to understand.

Children also react to pictures at a startlingly early age: Dorothy Butler's granddaughter Cushla, for instance, in one of the great longitudinal examinations of reading, responded to pictures and abstract symbols with fascination at nine months of age. Leonard Marcus argues that it can be appropriate to speak of "readers" of the picture, since a child's response to them is centered on words and names (35). In many books, especially alphabet books, art is simultaneously picture and language, as with Anno's Alphabet, Stephen Johnson's Alphabet City, and David Pelletier's The Graphic Alphabet. In a different vein, if you'll pardon the circulatory system pun, Ed Young's Voices of the Heart refigures the meaning of Chinese characters in new metaphoric images—in these books, the pictures are *about* language. From the child's point of view, the experience is no less reading for involving pictures. A toddler on a parent's lap experiencing Wild Things may not be literate in the technical sense of the term, but she is reading in the broad sense; she is decoding messages and meanings from the volume in front of her in order to recreate a story. Whether young children are poring over a wordless book, sharing a picture book read aloud, or privately experiencing both text and pictures, they are increasing their visual literacy and their understanding of the breadth and diversity of narrative.

FORMAT AND MORE

We often break up our discussion of picture books into the two components of words and pictures, but a recent spate of variations in form and physical effects reminds me that those aspects of a book, which don't fit neatly into the categories of words or pictures, also affect a narrative. Even before children can read books, the sheer physicality of a volume is very important to them; they are little inclined to abstract "text" or "pictures" from the construct of the book. Various studies have made it clear that physical makeup of a book greatly affects a child's response to it, and that children, who don't worry about shelving constraints, can warm to books both oversized and undersized. Children pet books and wear them, taste them and listen to them, creating a material connection with books that adults rarely envision. In reviewing Nodelman's *Words about Pictures*, Juliet Dusinberre reasonably criticizes him for failing to consider as a factor a book's smell (397); olfactory appeal rarely enters into critical discourse, but it can play a large part in a child's reaction. Maurice Sendak describes his reaction to a book received as a child:

> The first thing I did was to set it up on the table and stare at it for a long time. Not because I was impressed with Mark Twain; it was just a beautiful object. Then came the smelling of it. I think the smelling of books began with *The Prince and the Pauper*, because it was printed on particularly fine paper, unlike the Disney Big Little Books I had gotten previously, which were printed on very poor paper and smelled

poor. *The Prince and the Pauper* smelled good, and it also had a shiny cover, a laminated cover. I flipped over that. And it was solid. I mean, it was bound very tightly. I remember trying to bite it, which I don't imagine was what my sister had in mind when she bought the book for me. The last thing I did was to read it. It was all right. ("Notes" 173)

Sometimes these forms are variations of books originally published in a more traditional arrangement. Picture books get reissued as big books, for instance, and more and more of late turn up again in board book form. Pop-up versions have been around for awhile, but a new (or perhaps resurrected) form, so far used for original books only, has been the foldout frieze (or pullout panorama, as I note a new one calls itself), which accordion-folds neatly between the book covers but opens up into a single lengthy, connected page. Then, of course, there are the newer versions, the downloadable electronic text, or the book on CD-ROM. (There are also movies and television, but I'm speaking of forms in which the illustrative and the verbal text are the same as the original.)

I don't mean to suggest some sort of purist hierarchy, whereby the sewn binding and paper pages are some holy literary grail. I like board books, and popups, and CD-ROMs. Nor do I think the conversion of any book into a different format is a recipe for disaster. But the medium is at least part of the message, and a book's narrative alters with its format and appearance. The very way readers interact with the book is changed, which Beatrix Potter so wisely noted in specifying the tiny trim size of her volumes. A book you can make a clubhouse out of is obviously going to demand different treatment than a book you can tuck under your pillow, or one which can only be handled occasionally and gently. In her excellent *Horn Book* article, Sarah Ellis discusses some of the advantages and disadvantages of the electronic format of Bjarne Reuter's *The End of the Rainbow*, noting such important and overlookable details as the physical warmth of the laptop and its comparative unportability. [*Editor's note: The electronic format cited no longer was available at the time this publication went to press.*] A CD-ROM has its own momentum which can remove the onus from the reader. Scrolling is not the same as "the drama of the turning of the page," as Barbara Bader so eloquently puts it (1). This drama, too, is lost in the frieze, which offers a chance at a more sustained, less discretely episodic narrative, and indeed a more literally circular one. The story of snakes in *The Snake Book* would be a muted and lost one in a tiny format (though it might make a terrific frieze, with snakes all around). The focused and hemmed intensity of *Grandmother Bryant's Pocket* would lose its impact in a large trim size.

Working Together: Synthesis of Art Forms

But it's all got to come together somehow. Maurice Sendak, when discussing illustrating his own text, suggests that in order to attain this synthesis of art forms, a picture book creator not only deliberately balances the text and illustrations but "must not ever be doing the same thing, must not ever be illustrating exactly what you've written. You must leave a space in the text so the picture can do the work. Then you must come back to the word, and now the word does it best and the picture beats time. It's a funny kind of juggling act. It takes a lot of technique, a lot of experience, to really keep the rhythm going between word and picture" ("Notes" 185-86).

There's a story, for instance, about Katharine Hepburn and friends watching Charlie Chaplin's *A Countess from Hong Kong*, his big flop, and finding it awful. Then someone suggested turning the sound off, and they suddenly found it effective. Chaplin had written a successful visual narrative, as he had done so many times before, and then added superfluous words, creating an unsuccessful combination and an ultimately unsuccessful narrative. He had not performed what Sendak terms the balancing act.

Linda Ellerbee, discussing television news, suggests that if the news report makes equal sense without looking at the visuals, the program's doing it wrong, and that pictures that are merely redundant are superfluous. Dramatically speaking, there are a multitude of differences between television and picture books, particularly television news. But as Nodelman notes, television—like the picture book—is "a medium dependent upon the interrelationship of words and pictures. In his attack on wordless books, Patrick Groff suggests that, given the predominance of television in their lives, children are '"prewired" to see plots in pictures, but not in writing.' Given the predominance of television, I suspect that children are actually 'prewired' to see plots in pictures accompanied by words" (Nodelman 186). And the principle of pointless redundancy applies as well to both media; pictures may reinforce the text, but if they do only that, they are not using the medium to its fullest.

Text and pictures, in fact, can achieve remarkable effects in contradicting one another, expanding one another, or even limiting one another. Joseph Schwarcz speaks of Tomi Ungerer's pictures *as "spiting* the text" (16), and Perry Nodelman mentions that they are both narratives of dramatic irony (221), each speaking about matters on which the other is silent. He also notes the effect of illustrations not only in expanding the text but in opposing expansion, in buffering imagination and allowing it to explore dangerous areas in safety:

> When I have read the text of Sendak's *Where the Wild Things Are* to adults who have not previously heard it, without showing them the pictures, many feel it to be a terrifying story, too frightening for young children. Without Sendak's particular Wild Things to look at, they conjure up wild things out of their own nightmares, and those they find scary indeed. When I then tell them the story accompanied by the pictures, they always change their minds. (197)

Nor are the authorities of text and illustration identical. (We believe what we see, not what characters say—I just watched a show where we saw what the character did and then heard him deny it, which "means" that he's lying. How does that work? When did I learn this?) If, for instance, you see a television character saying one thing and pictures demonstrating another, the picture is generally "the truth." This can also be true in picture books, as in Stoeke's Minerva Louise series or Hutchins' *Rosie's Walk*—the pictures tell what really happened, and the text is just the concept the joke needs to contrast against. In Swiftian terms, the text is that which is not.

Yet there is room also for the illustrations to be their own kind of nonliteral truth, the truth, often, of the child protagonist. Whether you're talking about John Burningham's *Come Away from the Water, Shirley*, or Maggie Smith's *There's a Witch Under the Stairs*, the fact that the child's visions are pictured lends them credence. If *Where the Wild Things Are* pictured Max staring at the walls of his room or looking at a book of mythical beasts, it would be a book about the quaint imaginings of a thwarted child. In a genre, the picture book, where depiction of the legendary is commonplace and integral to the logic of many books, illustrations walk that narrow border between literal reality and imaginative reality, in a sense offering an authenticity that may not match objective experience.

It is partly out of the need for this balance that the best texts don't necessarily make the best picture book texts, and the best art doesn't necessarily make the best picture book illustration, just as the best poetry doesn't often make the best songs, and the Mona Lisa would have a hard time being an illustration of anything other than the Mona Lisa. When Christine Jenkins was describing the Graduate School of Library and Information Science's on-line classes, I was particularly intrigued by her ability to present picture books on the on-line environment with the text scrubbed out. And then I thought, with all the lovely neo-PhotoShop software available, that she could probably even fill in the text spaces or crop the pictures to present them as art that hadn't anything to do with words, and then I thought—maybe that's not quite fair? I'm reminded of Trina Schart Hyman, who responded to a gallery owner who lamented the empty blocks in the middle of her pictures, by stiffly pointing out that those empty blocks were the reason for the art. It's surprising, for instance, even in our small manipulation of images at the *Bulletin* (either selecting for the Web page or choosing art to include on our cover) how often impressive illustrations lose their thrill as mere art. I'm not suggesting that these separate elements must be deliberately bad in some way, but rather that works of art, whether literary or painterly, that are successful independently rarely have the skills, as it were, to be good partners.

Those partnerships can take a variety of forms. When Stephen Sondheim first started learning about the writing of musicals under the tutelage of Oscar Hammerstein, the master set his pupil certain tasks for his education. "For the first one," says Sondheim, "he told me to take a play I admired and turn it into a musical. . . . Next, he told me to take a play I didn't think was very good and could be improved and make a musical out of it. . . . For the third effort, Oscar told me to take something nondramatic, like a novel or a short story. . . . For the fourth and last in this series, he told me to write an original. . . " (Zadan 5). There are equivalents of those categories for picture books, too, and it's interesting to examine them when considering the relationship between the narratives. There are classic texts, such as Grimm and Perrault, that have been turned into picture books; there are not-so-classic texts that have been improved by their illustrations. Books such as James Michener's *South Pacific* are adaptations from another medium, and, of course, there is no lack of original books. Like musicals, picture books have components that are displayed independently and that sometimes are more successful separately than in their original setting. Yet together, the two aspects of those art forms are supposed to make something more than just the addition of the two, something greater than the sum of the parts and where the parts are no longer truly extricable from the whole. And surprisingly enough, they often do.

Like musicals, picture books almost always start with the text. This chronology is sufficiently established in the genre that books where the pictures have come first are rare indeed (though one cannot entirely be sure of the procedures of author-illustrators, whose prerogative it is to switch back and forth between the two). Often these art-first arrangements use pictures not to illustrate but to inspire, to take off from them as a starting point, such as Barbara Porte's riffs on Bill Traylor's art or Joan Aiken's stories from Jan Pienkowski's images. Sometimes, as in Walter Dean Myers' words for Jacob Lawrence's narrative paintings of the life of Toussaint L'Overture, the words undercut the carefully architected silent drama of the art when they are added to pictures made to be self-contained. Some of the most successful, such as Gwen Everett's *Li'l Sis and Uncle Willie* or Toyomi Igus' *Going Back Home* use the art not as expansion and illumination but as portraiture of people and situations within the story. Then there is the additional complication that, with some of these works, the art was originally designed to be substantially larger and hung on a wall; the collectiveness, intense focus, and smaller size of book art makes for an entirely different display situation, so even without the words, the art has become a different thing. These books demonstrate that even the chronology of words and pictures changes a narrative.

Whether or not they employ the traditional hierarchy of words and pictures, many picture books manage an extraordinary fusion of narratives into a read-aloud drama that is, as critic Peter Hunt notes, the only literary genre that children's literature contributes rather than borrows (175).

Nodelman states:

> Hearing someone else read a book, we are able to look at each picture during the whole time that the words printed with it are spoken.... Furthermore, hearing the words read aloud causes us to focus on them as a whole sequence—to want to know what happens next rather than to be content to pause and look at a picture when, for instance, a sentence has not been completed on a page. Children, then, encounter picture books when that literature is closest to its traditional ideal, but in a way far removed from most adults' reading experience. (263)

This is a unique effect. And to illustrate why it is worth taking pains to achieve, I go on one final borrowing mission, this time to Tom Stoppard's play *The Real Thing*. In the play, the character Henry, who is a writer, discusses the power of writing by using the metaphor of a cricket bat:

> This thing here, which looks like a wooden club, is actually several pieces of particular wood cunningly put together in a certain way so that the whole thing is sprung, like a dance floor. It's for hitting cricket balls with. If you get it right, the cricket ball will travel two hundred yards in four seconds, and all you've done is give it a knock like knocking the top off a bottle of stout, and it makes a noise like a trout taking a fly.... What we're trying to do is to write cricket bats, so that when we throw up an idea and give it a little knock, it might... *travel.* (53)

While literary physics may be a highly inexact science, we all know that it exists, and that properly formed picture books comprise several pieces of cunningly combined narrative to send those with which they connect a great distance. This is craftsmanship, and that is its goal. When all those pieces are put in place and they hit children at the right speed ... they travel.

WORKS CITED

Anno, Mitsumasa. *Anno's Alphabet: An Adventure in Imagination.* New York: HarperCollins, 1975.
—. *Anno's Journey.* New York: Philomel, 1978.
Bader, Barbara. *American Picturebooks: Noah's Ark to the Beast Within.* New York: MacMillan, 1976.
Briggs, Raymond. *Father Christmas.* London: Puffin, 1973.
—. *The Snowman.* London: H. Hamilton, 1978.
Burningham, John. *Come Away from the Water, Shirley.* New York: Crowell, 1977.
Butler, Dorothy. *Cushla and Her Books.* Boston: Horn Book, 1980.
A Countess from Hong Kong. Videocassette. Dir. Charlie Chaplin. MCA Universal Home Video, 1967. 108 min.
Dusinberre, Juliet. "Review of Perry Nodelman's *Words about Pictures.*" *Word and Image* 6.4 (1990): 396-97.
Elhert, Lois. *Circus.* New York: HarperCollins, 1992.
Ellerbee, Linda. *"And So It Goes:" Adventures in Television.* New York: Putnam's, 1986.
Ellis, Sarah. "Buster on the Screen." *The Horn Book Magazine* 73 (1997): 289-93.
Everett, Gwen. *Li'l Sis and Uncle Willie: A Story Based on the Life and Paintings of William H. Johnson.* Washington: National Museum of American Arts, 1991.

Fairy Tale: A True Story. Dir. Charles Sturbridge. Paramount, 1997.
Feelings, Tom. *The Middle Passage: White Ships/Black Cargo*. New York: Dial, 1995.
Friedrich, Priscilla. *The Easter Bunny that Overslept*. New York: Lothrop, Lee and Shepard, 1957.
Goldsmith, Evelyn. *Research into Illustration: An Approach and a Review*. Cambridge: Cambridge U P, 1984.
Groff, Patrick. "Children's Literature vs. Wordless 'Books.'" *Top of the News* (April 1974): 294-303.
Hunt, Peter. *Criticism, Theory, & Children's Literature*. Oxford: Blackwell, 1991.
Hutchins, Pat. *Rosie's Walk*. New York: Scholastic, 1968.
Hyman, Trina Schart. "Zen and the Art of Children's Book Illustration." *The Zena Sutherland Lectures, 1983-1992*. Ed. Betsy Hearne. New York: Clarion, 1993. 186-205.
Isadora, Rachel. *Ben's Trumpet*. New York: Greenwillow, 1979.
Igus, Toyomi. *Going Back Home: An Artist Returns to the South*. San Francisco: Children's Book Press, 1996.
Jenkins, Christine. Personal conversation. Undated.
Ling, Mary, Mary Atkinson, Frank Greenaway, and Dave King. *The Snake Book*. New York: DK, 1997.
Johnson, Stephen. *Alphabet City*. New York: Viking, 1995.
Marcus, Leonard S. "The Artist's Other Eye: The Picture Books of Mitsumasa Anno." *The Lion and the Unicorn* 7-8 (1983-84): 34-46.
Martin, Jacqueline Briggs. *Grandmother Bryant's Pocket*. Boston: Houghton, 1996.
Michener, James. *South Pacific*. San Diego: Harcourt, 1992.
Nodelman, Perry. *Words about Pictures: The Narrative Art of Children's Picture Books*. Athens, GA: The University of Georgia Press, 1988.
Pelletier, David. *The Graphic Alphabet*. New York: Orchard, 1996.
Rathmann, Peggy. *Good Night, Gorilla*. New York: Scholastic, 1994.
Reuter, Bjarne. *The End of the Rainbow*. Trans. Althea Bell. New York: Dutton, 1999.
Schwarcz, Joseph H. *Ways of the Illustrator: Visual Communication in Children's Literature*. Chicago: American Library Association, 1982.
Sendak, Maurice. *Caldecott & Co: Notes on Books and Pictures*. New York: Noonday/Farrar, Straus, Giroux, 1988.
—. *Where the Wild Things Are*. New York: Harper & Row, 1963.
Smith, Maggie. *There's a Witch Under the Stairs*. New York: Lothrop, Lee & Shepard, 1991.
Stoppard, Tom. *The Real Thing*. London: Faber and Faber, 1982.
Van Allsburg, Chris. *Jumanji*. Boston: Houghton, 1981.
—. *The Sweetest Fig*. Boston: Houghton, 1993.
Willard, Nancy. *A Visit to William Blake's Inn: Poems for Innocent and Experienced Travelers*. New York: Harcourt, 1981.
Young, Ed. *Voices of the Heart*. New York: Scholastic, 1997.
Zadan, Craig. *Sondheim & Co*. Rev. ed. New York: Da Capo, 1994.

DEBORAH STEVENSON
Associate Editor
The Bulletin of the Center for Children's Books
Graduate School of Library and Information Science
University of Illinois at Urbana-Champaign

Construction, Illustration, and a Plethora of Pigs: Reflections on a Lecture by Arthur Geisert[*]

It's a measure of the power of storytelling, I suppose, or at least the power of Arthur Geisert's storytelling, that after two days of intense concentration on the topic of story we were still seduced into rapt attention by closed curtains, dimmed lights, and a well-turned tale. In this case, however, the tale was autobiographical and accompanied by slides, describing the Geiserts' Herculean labors in the construction of two charming and almost entirely inaccessible homes as well as Mr. Geisert's work in picture books.

Even without the literary connection, the Great Building Saga would have made a gripping narrative; one hopes the Geiserts found it as amusing at the time as they managed to make it seem in retrospect. Both the house constructed atop a forested and trackless hill (it looked like a mountain in the pictures, but we're not supposed to have mountains in Illinois) and the elegant yet appealingly Rube Goldbergesque structure in the old quarry were infinitely desirable artistic eyries and thrilling to contemplate, but perhaps even more thrilling was the safe distance between us in the audience and the labor of their building process.

As Mr. Geisert's slides made clear, these were not merely significant and backbreaking aspects of his life, but experiences that were the source for much of his art. Obviously the man had peculiar insight into Noah's ark-building travails, for one thing; more important, however, was the realization that his literary pigs's bent for construction came from that of their maker. When the D pigs in *Pigs from A to Z* drag lumber, pulling together as a team and relaying around a pulley-tree, it isn't just a porcine way around the problem of hooves or a conveniently alliterative action, but an echo of a Geisert construction scene. When the pigs of *Pigs from 1 to 10* build a bridge across a gorge, they're simply following Geisert's real-life

*Arthur Geisert's art is reprinted by permission of Houghton Mifflin Company.

D is for dragging the lumber. Dragging was drudgery. (*Pigs from A to Z*, p. 15)

80　STORY: FROM FIREPLACE TO CYBERSPACE

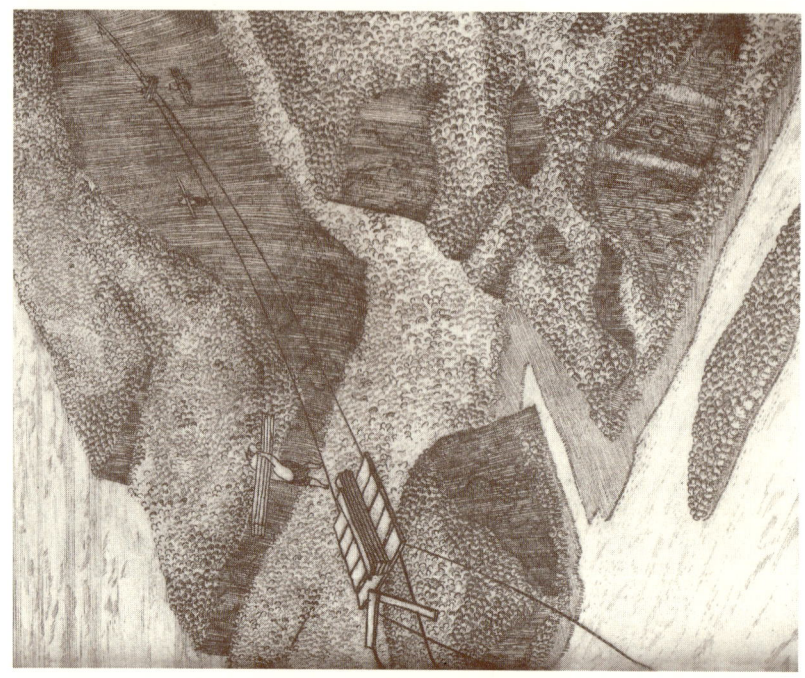

Balancing carefully, we built a bridge. (Pigs from 1 to 10, pp. 16 and 17)

example (which leads one to wonder if there isn't somewhere a pig building houses and illustrating books showing teams of laboring Geiserts).

The places Geisert made are, of course, not only the places in his art but the places wherein that art is created. This was made brutally clear by the photograph of a huge press being hauled up the hillside through the trees, looking like the scene from *Burden of Dreams* documenting the dragging of a Spanish-galleon replica through the Peruvian jungle. This is also reflected in his book *The Etcher's Studio*, which shows a workplace that, like etcher Geisert's studio, is chock-a-block with the tools of the trade and the fruits—and the pigs—of his labor. Fortunately both the construction and artistic labor have been well worth the effort: Geisert is an artist who knows construction, whether it be of an etching or a house among the rocks, and who seemingly takes as much pleasure in the process as in the product. He lives in both kinds of creations, since slides of his studio show the illustrations he made lining the walls of this room in the house he made, and his stories about the one construction become the stories within the other.

WORKS CITED

Burden of Dreams. Videocassette. Dir. Les Blank. Flower Films, 1982. 94 min.
Geisert, Arthur. *The Etcher's Studio.* Boston: Houghton, 1997.
—. *Pigs from A to Z.* Boston: Houghton, 1986.
—. *Pigs from 1 to 10.* Boston: Houghton, 1992.

I helped him get ready. (*The Etcher's Studio*, p. 5)

Section Four: Story as Institutional Culture

Both of the presentations that end this collection speak to concerns for the future of stories and storytelling. In the past, the only way to know a story was to hear it, to be connected to it by blood or proximity. As literacy evolved, traditional stories were captured, indeed rescued from oblivion, by the collectors and folklorists who gathered stories in print form. Now stories span huge distances via many forms of media, and children in the U.S. can go to their local library—or to the vast reaches of cyberspace—and read and hear stories from Brazil or the Philippines, from Vietnam or Russia or Nigeria. The ones they love they may tell or enact or reread. Thus stories go from print to oral and back again. This an activity that has kept, and continues to keep, stories alive. And libraries provide the stories that fuel this interaction for current and future generations of children and of storytellers. Children's librarians are certainly not the only storytellers out there, but by virtue of their role in both the promotion of stories and of reading, their collections become the gateway through which the child can enter the world of story again and again.

Christine Jenkins' essay reminds us that stories and storytelling are not only part of humankind's past and present, but part of our future as well. Stories—whether ancient, modern, postmodern, or only a gleam in a storyteller's eye—survive. Janice Del Negro's essay, actually a speech inspired by the 39th Allerton Conference (thus, included here) and given a week later as the keynote address at the Champaign Public Library Children's Literature Conference, reminds us of both the "how" and the "why" of helping children make this essential connection.

CJ

CHRISTINE JENKINS
Assistant Professor
Graduate School of Library and Information Science
University of Illinois at Urbana-Champaign

The Cycle of Story: From Fireplace to Marketplace or, "The Kids Keep Tearing Their Jeans"

In considering the cycle of story from fireplace to marketplace, we begin a journey from the domestic to the commercial, from private to public space, from the priceless human interaction of the story and the listener to the commercial transaction of the product and the consumer. If stories are to reach a larger audience, a consideration of the stories of the fireplace must include a consideration of the marketplace.

Those of us whose work includes stories will acknowledge that communicating our stories to audiences beyond the sound of our voices involves publishing those stories. Publishing, however, requires money, which generally involves convincing an editor and a marketing department that their company will make money (i.e., a profit) from our product. Perhaps not a lot of money, but money nonetheless. And money, as both Karl Marx and Cyndi Lauper have so eloquently put it, changes everything.

While stories are for all ages—with some audiences and tellers receiving more respect than others—the specific focus in this paper is the path from fireplace to marketplace as it applies to telling and publishing stories for a young audience—i.e., for children. The path is a problematic one for many. Despite the fact that we know that money makes many worlds go round, there is something about story as commodity, about putting a price tag on imagination, about the juxtaposition of concerns of children and of money, that makes many people extremely uncomfortable. This is true in the advanced capitalism of contemporary American society. This was equally true a century ago in the early years of American youth services librarianship. This is a profession with a long history of hostility toward the concept of story as commodity.

Effie L. Power's textbook *Library Service for Children* was published in 1930 by the American Library Association; the text (and its 1943 revision, *Work with Children in Public Libraries*) was considered "the" text in the training of children's librarians throughout the 1930s and 1940s. Power devoted several pages of the section on book selection to "fiction which fails to meet accepted standards," by which she meant the children's mass market series book (72). She condemned them as "books which cater to the lazy minded. . . . easily detected by their hackneyed plots, wooden style, and lifeless characters" (73). Power illustrated these qualities with a critique of a representative book of the genre, *The Bobbsey Twins and Their Schoolmates*, noting that the book ("the 21st book of a mediocre series") contains an appendix that "calls attention to **other** titles in several long series" [emphasis in original] (73). While the story's ostensible purpose was clearly entertainment, Power stated "an ulterior purpose is suggested by specific reference to other books in the series" (74). The ulterior purpose was, of course, the promotion and sale of more books. And Power is adamant: "Obviously a book of this type has no place in children's reading" (75). Though the rhetoric has softened considerably since that time (one oft-cited anti-series salvo, Mary E.S. Root's 1929 article in *Wilson Library Bulletin*, was titled simply "Not to Be Circulated"), condemnations of mass market series books have continued to appear in the literature of youth services librarianship from that day to this. The series' lack of literary quality is the reason usually cited for librarians' negative view of series books, but along with that has been children's librarians' traditional rejection of story as commodity, of made-to-order texts for children marketed as "product."   This division is not limited to children's publishing but is found throughout the book industry in the ongoing tension between culture and commerce, between texts as literature and texts as product (Coser).

It is understandably galling to children's librarians to spend even a part of their inadequate book budgets on series books that they know are manufactured solely to make a profit, each with its extra pages devoted to advertising more of the same, plus (as with the Baby-Sitters Club series) board games, charm bracelets, calendars, dolls, videos, and fan club membership. At the same time, the demand is certainly there. And reading research consistently identifies a strong positive correlation between children's series book reading and their later development into fluent adult readers (Carlsen 44-55; Carlsen and Sherrill 87-94). And yet . . . the idea that a children's story is simply one more saleable commodity continues to disturb those who are concerned with the preservation and perpetuation of story. And not just any story, but good stories, worthwhile stories, authentic stories, stories that nourish children's hearts and inspire their imaginations, the stories in the sort of books that Paul Hazard was referring to when he wrote, "'Give us books,' say the children, 'give us wings. You who are powerful and strong, help us to escape into the faraway. . . . We are willing to learn everything that we are taught at school, but, please, let us keep our dreams'" (4). While this cry may or may not be a notion more romantic than realistic, picturing a children's book as just another kind of widget to promote and sell, viewing young people as simply another group of consumers, their imaginations dulled by stories packaged and rewritten for the broadest audience appeal—these are troubling images.

When stories go to the marketplace is it possible for them not to slide down that very slippery slope to bland—or garish—commercialization, that place where it is impossible not to be blinded by the bottom line? What is "the integrity of a story"? If tellers and writers have one eye on the marketplace as they make a traditional story their own, have they sold out? These are vital questions for those of us whose work involves connecting young people with stories. And because we are living in a present filled with media tie-ins and television shows that are nothing more than half-hour commercials for story-linked action figures, breakfast cereal and computer games, one may be forgiven for thinking that things could hardly get worse, that young people's minds will inevitably (and irrevocably) be corrupted by market forces. And what will our world look like when popular culture becomes the only culture, the only game in town?

THE GRIMMS AT THE MARKETPLACE

Despite the age-old feeling that present problems are far worse than past ones, there are useful parallels to be made between current struggles with the impact of capitalism on today's stories and past struggles along the road from the fireplace to the marketplace. One such struggle occurred in Germany during the late eighteenth century, a time when a great number of small independent states were in the process of unifying under a common government—a process that came very late in comparison to other European countries. This was a time marked by great political tension. There was tension between France and Germany, recently exacerbated by Napoleon's occupation of German land. There were also tensions between and among the many German-speaking jurisdictions as they moved, contentiously and reluctantly, toward unification. Not coincidentally, this was also the time of the Heidelberg Romantic Movement and its emphasis on German culture as a unique entity—the product of a single Germanic Volk—a movement that inspired the collecting of German folksongs, legends, and stories, as well as the birth and growth of German nationalism (Zipes, "Breaking" 70; Bottigheimer, "Bad Girls" 3-6).

Jacob and Wilhelm Grimm were Germans born in 1785 and 1786, the two oldest sons of the six children of Philipp Wilhelm Grimm, a magistrate who died in 1895, when Jacob and Wilhelm were eleven and ten years old. Their father's death reduced the family's resources and status, and Jacob and Wilhelm were well aware that their career success would be important to the welfare of their mother and siblings. They left home for school in Kassel in 1898 and from there went to the University of Marburg to study law. While in Marburg, they became increasingly interested in the study of old German literature and became involved in the Heidelberg Romantic Movement. At the same time they wrote and sought to publish scholarly work that would contribute to the support of their family (Zipes, "Dreams" 206-213). In 1805-08, two Heidelberg scholars and writers, Clemens Brentano and Achim von Arnim, compiled, edited, and published one of the earliest collections of German folksongs, *Des Knaben Wunderhorn* (*The Youth's Wonderhorn*) (Ellis 7). The Grimm brothers assisted in this work, and four years later began compiling and editing a fairy tale collection that would be a record of German oral tradition for an adult and scholarly audience. With the help of Arnim, the Grimms published the first of two volumes of *Kinder- und Haus-Märchen* (*Nursery and Household Tales*) in 1812, the second volume in 1815 (Tatar 6).

There is a common but mistaken image of the Grimms as anthropologists of sorts, traveling about the countryside, stopping in villages to hear the stories of German peasants. This, however, was not the case; the Grimms did not gather their stories "in the field" (or, more accurately, in that picturesque—and imaginary—rural field) but from lower-middle and middle class urban women (such as Dorothea Viehmann, Marie and Jeannette Hassenpflug, and Dorchen Wild) who were skilled storytellers (Scherf 183-189). Along with many others, the Grimms believed that folktales—whether told in a hut or a drawing room—revealed "the true heart of the Volk." As scholars of linguistics and philology, they considered their work a scientific, rather than a popular, collection and included notes on sources and variants (Degh 68-70).

The Grimms edited their tales (and continued to edit their tales) from the first publication in 1812 to the final 1857 edition. The reviews of that first, scholarly edition were mixed, as critics welcomed this expression of the German volk spirit but deplored the tales' inappropriateness for children. Even friendly reviewers, such as Clemens Brentano, criticized the Grimms' adherence to oral tradition at the expense of reader comfort; Brentano wrote, "If you want to display children's clothing you can do that quite well without bringing out an outfit that has buttons torn off it, dirt smeared on it, and the shirt hanging out of the pants," while Arnim suggested that they add a subtitle that would be a "parental guidance" warning: "for parents, who can select stories for retelling" (Tatar 16).

There is no question that the Grimms were aware that the marketplace value of their collection would increase considerably if the tales were made "suitable for children." At that time Jacob and Wilhelm were supporting two of their younger brothers. In addition, the financial incentive was considerable: projected royalties for the edition were 500 talers, a sum roughly equivalent to each of the brothers' yearly income. As literary scholar Maria Tatar noted, "the Grimms may never have made or even hoped to make a financial killing on the *Nursery and Household Tales*, but the profit motive was certainly not wholly absent from their calculations and to some extent must have guided their revisions [on the first edition]" (14). Indeed, with an eye to their audience, the second edition's introduction stated: "we have thus eliminated in this edition any expression that is not suitable for childhood" (Ward 95). In this new expurgated (and certainly less authentic) edition, sexual references were eliminated and violence was confined to that which made sense in a moral world: the good were rewarded, the bad punished, with punishments growing progressively harsher and more detailed as the editions continued to be edited and published. Increasingly, the tales emphasized correct morals, manners, and behavior; the value of diligence and the value of hard work; beauty linked to virtue; and national pride (Tatar 28-33).

Kinder- und Haus-Märchen went through a total of 17 editions from 1812 to 1857, when the final edition was published. The first and second editions sold moderately well. In 1823, however, translator Edgar Taylor published an illustrated children's edition of a selection of Grimms' tales in English that was a popular and commercial success (Bottigheimer, "Bad Girls" 10, 19). Noting this success, Wilhelm Grimm compiled and edited an illustrated edition of 50 of the best-known tales that was published in 1825. The text was illustrated (by their brother Ludwig) and further revised specifically for a young audience. It was this "Small Edition," which contained Snow White, The Frog King, Hansel and Gretel, Cinderella, Little Red Riding Hood, Rumplestiltskin and other now-familiar stories, that became a popular bestseller. In the years that followed, the Grimms published further editions of the tales and in 1850, the Grimms' tales became part of the Prussian elementary school curriculum. Grimms' tales went on to become part of curriculum of all German schools, where they were read and studied by every German school child through the end of the Second World War (Bottigheimer, "Bad Girls" 21).

The Grimms made few public statements about their expurgation, consistently describing the changes they made as ones that brought the story "closer to the original." It is clear, however, that the Grimms were also editing with an awareness of the youth of their primary audience. As Grimms scholar Maria Tatar has pointed out, "Wilhelm Grimm rewrote the tales so extensively and went so far in the direction of eliminating off-color episodes that he can be credited with sanitizing folktales and thereby paving the way for the process that made them acceptable children's literature in all cultures" (24). Indeed, the Grimms were among those who led the way to the cultural riches in the tales of the fireplace; and their interest in the actual riches to be had in refashioning the tales for young audiences led the way to the marketplace as well.

Making Stories Suitable for Children

"Suitable for children" continues to be a key factor in turning a story into a product—the seemingly inevitable transformation/transmogrification of figurative cultural capital to literal cultural capital. And it was into this complex process that Power and other children's librarians inserted themselves as arbiters in discerning and promoting "the rarest kind of best" in stories for young people. But acting in this role does not mean we are immune to the tension between the questions, "Is this story an authentic representation of a culture's narrative voice(s)?" and "Will this story sell? And, if not, can (should?) something (anything?) be done to transform the story, to give it more 'curb appeal'?"

Sometimes these changes and transformations appear to be thoughtless cultural erasures, as in William Sleator's *The Angry Moon*, a Caldecott Honor book that combines a Tlingit Indian tale with narrative conventions of European folklore, using three rather than four as a mythic number. Someone apparently thought that this change was an improvement, but what was the original story? And what else might have been altered to make this a story for mainstream Western audiences?

Sometimes these changes appear as deliberate expurgation, as with Charlotte Huck's text for *Princess Furball*, a variant of the Grimms tale "Allerleirauh" ("Thousandfurs"), the story of a king determined to marry his daughter, who responds by fleeing to a neighboring kingdom. Huck changed the story to eliminate any reference to incest (in her telling, the girl runs away because her father has ordered her to marry an ogre). From this point, the story's plot proceeds more or less like the original, but Huck's editing has in fact changed the characters of both the girl and her father, which in turn changes the entire logic of the story. The tale becomes more "suitable for children," but at what cost?

Sometimes tellers (including ourselves) change stories to reflect the folk motifs that are an integral part of our own personal schema of "the way things ought to be." We do this not only with folklore from other cultures, but with our personal stories as well. We tell and retell our stories, creating and recreating the meanings we have ascribed to the stories that are our lives. It is, after all, painfully disconcerting to feel that our life experiences are directed in part by chance, by the chaotic movement of people, by small and large events beyond our control, by wars and treaties, good and bad harvests, disease and health, poverty and wealth. And that these factors, whether random or preordained, have converged to put all of us here in this place at this present moment.

We want roots, we want to feel like we are standing on solid ground. And our stories give us that foundation. There is a sense in which our stories, our individual narratives, are the most personal, the most intimate entities in our lives. Even in our dreams we turn what may be simply the random firing of neurons into a story. Regardless of how much or how little sense a dream makes, it is still a story, it is still our story, a story that only we will ever experience.

There is a terrible indignation about the people who sell a culture's stories; who sell our stories; who sell our stories and get them wrong who sell our stories and get them wrong but because there are 10,000 print copies of their version and only a single oral version of our story, their story "wins" and becomes "the" story. And what could be more infuriating than to watch as an oral narrative—a story that is owned by everyone and no one—is claimed as one person's intellectual property, copyrighted, and sold. We get no money in this transaction, so we can only feel deprived. Do we lose when our stories are turned into commodities? And if so, what exactly is it that we have lost?

Stories in the Marketplace

In the chaos and glitz of the marketplace, we get stories, stories, and more stories, churned out like so many Franklin Mint collectibles, while the Opies' masterful children's folklore collection *I Saw Esau* (with illustrations by Maurice Sendak!) sits on the remainder table at Borders. Multiple versions of the Grimms' tales continue to proliferate, but, as Betsy Hearne noted in her survey of in-print editions of Sleeping Beauty, most of the texts she examined display an indifference on the part of authors and illustrators to the tale's sources or internal logic—evidently the publishers' motivations "must have been marketing potential rather than aesthetic or psychological appreciation of the story's value" (233). And when young people ask for the "real" version of Snow White, what they are asking for is not the Grimms' tale but Grumpy, Dopey, Sneezy, Happy, Sleepy, Bashful, and Doc. The Disney version has become "the real version."

The monolith of popular culture embodied in mass market narratives like Goosebumps, Power Rangers, and Sweet Valley High seems so large and powerful and children so small and powerless. But what do children do with that mass market "real version" once they acquire it in print or in other media—in comic, video, game, or action figure? The story of children and popular culture in print or plastic, audio or visual, doesn't end at the cash register.

In his book, *Understanding Popular Culture*, cultural theorist John Fiske uses the image and the actuality of blue jeans to make some observations about the dynamic nature of popular mass market culture in his essay, "The Jeaning of America." Clothing has long been a signifier of various meanings to both the wearer and the observer. At one time jeans were an item of apparel that signified rebellion; now they are ubiquitous, worn by members of a range of classes and cultures. Despite the apparent commonality, however, wearers of jeans—particularly young people—will often purchase their ready-to-wear jeans and then immediately change them to create their own self-representation that may be decidedly different from the look that Ralph Lauren or Liz Claiborne had in mind.

If today's jeans are to express oppositional meanings, or even to gesture toward such social resistance, they need to be disfigured in some way—tie-dyed, irregularly bleached, or, particularly, torn. If "whole" jeans connote shared meanings of contemporary America, then disfiguring them becomes a way of distancing oneself from those values . . . at the simplest level, this is an example of a user not simply consuming a commodity but reworking it, treating it not as a completed object to be accepted passively, but as a cultural resource to be used (Fiske 4, 10).

The free market economy of the late twentieth century is characterized by a seemingly endless cycle of manufactured commodities that are advertised and sold to consumers, whose money provides both paychecks and profit statements to workers and owners, respectively. But focusing solely on the process of supplying commodities to customers obscures the meanings of those commodities from the perspective of the consumer. And not simply consumers as subjects of market research, but consumers as creators of their own meanings. And much as producers would like to control the meanings their products have for their customers, the fact is, they cannot. In the case of jeans, when manufacturers saw that young people were washing, bleaching, and ripping their jeans, they began producing "factory-made tears, or by 'washing' or fading jeans in the factory before sale. This process of adopting the signs of resistance incorporates them into the dominant system and thus attempts to rob them of any oppositional meanings" (Fiske 18). But as soon as faded jeans appear on the clothing racks at the Gap or at Target, young jeans wearers begin to alter those jeans to create a new modification, a new Look. And so it goes.

Popular culture always is part of power relations; it always bears traces of the constant struggle between domination and subordination, between power and various forms of resistance to it or evasions of it, between military strategy and guerrilla tactics. Evaluating the balance of power within this struggle is never easy: Who can say, at any one point, who is "winning" a guerilla war? The essence of guerilla warfare, as of popular culture, lies in not being defeatable. Despite nearly two centuries of capitalism, subordinated subcultures exist and intransigently refuse finally to be incorporated—people in these subcultures keep devising new ways of tearing their jeans (Fiske 19).

It is common knowledge that a handful of giant corporations dominate the communications industry, both nationally and internationally. ABC is a subsidiary of Disney, which also owns theme parks, an oil and gas company, cable channels, magazines, newspapers, record companies, an insurance company, and even a hockey team. Time Warner owns Turner Broadcasting, parent company of CNN, as well as sports teams, cable companies, film studios, and retail stores. NBC is now owned by GE, while CBS belongs to Westinghouse. Fox Television is part of Rupert Murdoch's media empire, which also includes HarperCollins publishing, newspapers, magazines, and television stations. Not surprisingly, many observers worry about the impact of having so many channels of communication controlled by a small number of mega-corporations.

It is difficult not to worry about the impact this "literary-industrial complex" will have on our democratic future (West 1-7). As one of the many who are dedicated to the promotion of quality texts representing a diversity of viewpoints to young readers, this is certainly one of my worries. But just when I think that corporations really are on the verge of success as they strive to turn people into consumer automatons, that they really have cracked the code for how to get us to want whatever it is they have to sell and reject anything not previously seen on television, I consider the folk culture that surrounds us. In the apprehension generated by the Big Picture, it is important to remember the Small Picture as well, by which I mean the folk culture that is part of our everyday lives and, for the purposes of this paper, the everyday lives of children.

The image of traditional folk culture pictures the individual or the group fashioning meaningful objects from natural materials, meaningful stories from their observations of the heavens, the earth, the oceans, the weather, and other natural phenomena. But manufactured objects, urban landscapes, and mass media can also be used by the individual and the group as raw materials from which to fashion their own meanings and culture that may or may not be quite different from those ascribed by the corporate creators of those objects or that media. Fiske describes this creation of popular culture as "necessarily the art of making do with what is available" (15). In earlier times, "what is available" might be leaves or pebbles or bamboo or animal skins. Contemporary folk artists may use bottle caps or broken china or discarded tires or styrofoam cups. In our throw-away culture, there is always something available. And who knows this better than children?

CHILDREN, HALLOWEEN COSTUMES, AND THE FOLK PROCESS

Ready-made Halloween costumes depicting the mass media characters most popular with children in a given year are one example that is used as evidence of the deterioration of the pure and innocent ghosts and pirates, hobos and monsters, witches and princesses from when we were children. As one adult, a package designer for Hasbro Toys, stated, "What kids want and what they fantasize about is just a regurgitation of what they've seen on TV. It's scary, that their fantasies are so controlled by the media, and what adults think will sell to kids. And Halloween's just more of the same" (Jenkins 1). However, in my research into children's Halloween costume choices and aesthetics, I found that the plastic costumes off the rack at K-Mart are really not a threat to the folk process. If we take a close look at the lives of many young people in contemporary U.S. culture during the final weeks of October, we will see that—both figuratively and literally—children continue to tear their jeans.

I conducted my research among the 300-plus students, age 5 to 12, of a single elementary school in Ann Arbor, Michigan, where I conducted group and individual interviews during the week before Halloween. I asked children to describe their costumes for the current and for past years, their decision-making process for determining their costume choice, and their standards for what they thought constituted a good costume or a poor one.

The answers I got fell into distinct patterns according to the age of the child. The children described by the Hasbro employee, who "just want to be what they see on TV," were the youngest: preschoolers, kindergartners, and some first-graders. They are great fans of television superhero cartoon shows and their play often involved those characters. By the time most students were in first grade, however, many saw store-bought superhero costumes as babyish, with some even claiming to hate their old cartoon favorites. Many of them consulted their parents in choosing a costume, which might very well be an older sibling's former costume, but most felt that they themselves had final say on their choice. Children in first and second grade might have an adult/parent-created costume—an E.T. with every line and wrinkle sewn in, for example, or a knight with elaborate cardboard armor, or a Cinderella in a miniature ball gown. But they were beginning to place greater importance on creating at least some part of their own costume themselves. By third grade, nearly all students viewed Halloween costumes as not simply a requirement for peer acceptance or trick-or-treating, but as a self-created signifier of some aspect of their identity. This could be a weighty decision; one boy described his decision-making process: "Right now my mind is racing between a devil and a lumberjack" (Jenkins 4). They were inspired by other costumes, by peers, by television shows, comics, books, favorite activities, or future aspirations. They might be a doctor, or a tennis star, or a character out of a favorite comic book, or one of the more traditional choices of pirate, hobo, witch, gypsy, ghost, etc.

The oldest elementary students (fourth and fifth graders) placed great importance on making or putting their costume together themselves. They might ask for some small amount of help from parents, but only after they had already decided what they would be. They took particular delight in describing what I call collage objects, such as lion paws created out of gardening gloves and stick-on fingernails, or frog's eyes made from ping pong balls. All of these involved taking familiar objects and reconfiguring them to create something new. Borrowing an older sibling's hair mousse, a younger sibling's stuffed tiger, and becoming Calvin of "Calvin and Hobbes," was just exactly right to them. In fashioning their own costumes the older students, who were as avid as young students in their consumption of popular culture, consistently rejected the mass customization of a manufactured costume in favor of the "homemade" costume, that is, one designed and created by and for themselves. So what did these older children make of the off-the-rack versions of Spiderman, Pocahontas, Hercules, and the Little Mermaid? "Oh well, those are really for little kids" (Jenkins 9).

Overall, the students placed a high value on personal choice in costumes, no matter how rudimentary the result. Given this fact, it is hardly surprising that store-bought costumes are most popular with young children. They want some choice, but most are not old enough to be able to assemble a costume themselves. Their best compromise is a ready-to-wear costume that they pick out themselves from among a store display of other such costumes. Hence the brief but intense attraction of costumes from K-Mart for preschoolers and kindergartners. The folk process survives another onslaught from those who would turn everything they could sell into commodities.

It is the same with story, whether it is an explanation of how the sun and moon came to live in the sky, or why mosquitoes buzz in people's ears, or how our great-grandparents came to America, or what Godzilla does when he's not terrorizing Tokyo, or who used to live in the house next door. Stories are pieced together from the old and the new, are created and recreated over and over again, and no matter how much Disney Studios wants their version of Beauty and the Beast to be "the" version, no matter how many media tie-ins they license, the underlying story is not static. With or without permissions, we take it and use it; we act it out with Barbies and stuffed animals; we refashion it to tell to our children, our students, or our therapists; we take a piece of this version and a piece of that version, a piece of Jo March and Professor Bhaer, a piece of *Daddy Longlegs*, and perhaps even a piece of our own lives; we take it and change it and use it and make it ours. The children keep tearing their jeans. And so, I hope, will we.

Works Cited

Arnim, Ludwig Achim von and Clemens Brentano, comps. *Des Knaben Wunderhorn: Alte Deutsche Lieder.* 3 vols. Heidelberg: Mohr u. Zimmer, Breitkopf und Härtel, 1805-08.

Bottigheimer, Ruth B., ed. *Fairy Tales and Society: Illusion, Allusion, and Paradigm.* Philadelphia: U of Pennsylvania P, 1986.

—. *Grimms' Bad Girls and Bold Boys: The Moral and Social Vision of the Tales.* New Haven: Yale U P, 1987.

Carlsen, G. Robert. *Books and the Teenage Reader: A Guide for Teachers, Librarians, and Parents.* 2nd rev. ed. New York: Bantam, 1980.

Carlsen, G. Robert and Anne Sherrill. *Voices of Readers: How We Come to Love Books.* Urbana: NCTE, 1988.

Coser, Lewis, Charles Kadushin, and Walter P. Powell. *Books: The Culture and Commerce of Publishing.* Chicago: U of Chicago P, 1985.

Degh, Linda. "What Did the Grimm Brothers Give to and Take from the Folk?" *The Brothers Grimm and Folktale.* Ed. James M. McGlathery. Urbana: U of Illinois P, 1988. 66-90.

Ellis, John M. *One Fairy Story Too Many: The Brothers Grimm and Their Tales.* Chicago: U of Chicago P, 1983.

Fiske, John. *Understanding Popular Culture.* London: Routledge, 1991.

Grimm, Jacob and Wilhelm Grimm, comp. *Kinder- und Haus-Märchen.* 2 vols. Berlin: Realschulbuchhandlung, 1812/1815.
Hazard, Paul. *Books, Children, and Men.* Boston: Horn Book, 1944.
Hearne, Betsy. "Booking the Brothers Grimm: Art, Adaptations, and Economics." *The Brothers Grimm and Folktale.* Ed. James M. McGlathery. Urbana: U of Illinois P, 1988. 220-33.
Hope, Laura Lee. *The Bobbsey Twins and Their Schoolmates.* New York: Grosset & Dunlap, 1918.
Huck, Charlotte S. *Princess Furball.* New York: Greenwillow, 1989.
Jenkins, Christine. "Dressed to Fool: An Investigation into the Folklore of Children's Halloween Costumes." Unpublished paper, 1988.
Lauper, Cyndi. "Money Changes Everything." *She's So Unusual.* Portrait, BFR 38930, 1983.
Opie, Iono Archibald and Peter Opie. *I Saw Esau: The Schoolchild's Pocketbook.* Cambridge: Candlewick, 1992.
Power, Effie L. *Library Service for Children.* Chicago: ALA, 1930.
—. *Work with Children in Public Libraries.* Chicago: ALA, 1943.
Root, Mary E.S. "Not to Be Circulated: A List, Prepared by Mrs. E.S. Root, of Books in Series Not Circulated by Standardized Libraries." *Wilson Library Bulletin* 3 (1929): 446.
Scherf, Walter. "Jacob and Wilhelm Grimm: A Few Small Corrections to a Commonly Held Image." *The Brothers Grimm and Folktale.* Ed. James M. McGlathery. Urbana: U of Illinois P, 1988. 178-91.
Sleator, William. *The Angry Moon.* Boston: Little, Brown, 1970.
Tatar, Maria. *The Hard Facts of the Grimms' Fairy Tales.* Princeton, NJ: Princeton U P, 1987.
Ward, Donald. "New Misconceptions about Old Folktales: The Brothers Grimm." *The Brothers Grimm and Folktale.* Ed. James M. McGlathery. Urbana: U of Illinois P, 1988. 91-100.
West, Celeste. *The Passionate Perils of Publishing.* San Francisco: Booklegger Press, 1978.
Zipes, Jack. *Breaking the Magic Spell: Radical Theories of Folk and Fairy Tales.* Austin: U of Texas P, 1979.
—. "Dreams of a Better Bourgeois Life: The Psychosocial Origins of the Grimms' Tales." *The Brothers Grimm and Folktale.* Ed. James M. McGlathery. Urbana: U of Illinois P, 1988. 205-19.

WORKS CONSULTED

Haugland, Ann. "The Crack in the Old Canon: Culture and Commerce in Children's Books." *The Lion and the Unicorn* 18 (June 1994): 48-59.

JANICE M. DEL NEGRO
Editor
The Bulletin of the Center for Children's Books
Graduate School of Library and Information Science
University of Illinois at Urbana-Champaign

For Story's Sake: Reading as its Own Reward

We live in a media-saturated society that, on a surface level at least, increasingly defines individuals by their outer trappings: how they look, the goods they have, the stuff they can afford to buy, the toys they play with. We live in an era that rewards the quick fix, the easy answer, and the software solution; in a time when the words "long term," "delayed gratification," and "whatever is worth doing is worth doing well" are considered anachronistic at best and laughable at worst. Michael Millken goes to jail for a white collar crime and comes out a multimillionaire; honesty is cynically equated with stupidity, and ethics are situational and malleable. Nobody does anything for nothing, if you don't take care of yourself no one else will, and it serves you right for being such a sentimental fool. The bottom line is all that matters, whether in budget or circulation figures—if you can't measure it, it's not valuable—and kids need to be paid off with bribes and incentives in order to participate in reading programs or other book-related activities. If they're not, reading program participation figures will go down, circulation figures will plummet, and book-buying budgets will dwindle accordingly.

How's that for a scenario? Nuclear winter is cozier.

I love books. I have always loved them. I have no memory of a time when I did not know how to read. My first memory of actually reading a book is the poems in *The Pocket Book of Verse*. I think it belonged to my older brother. "Tyger, tyger burning bright,/ in the forests of the night;/ what immortal hand or eye,/ could frame thy fearful symmetry?" (Blake Pl. 42). Or, "Take her up tenderly, lift her with care, fashioned so slenderly, young and so fair" (Hood 274). And, "Young Lochinvar is come out of the West,/Through all the wide Border his steed was the best. . . " (Scott 130). Did I know what they meant? I didn't have a clue. And it didn't matter.

I inadvertently stumbled through the door of the public library and found solace and sustenance—in silence, in books, in language. The public library was an incredible haven, a respite from a world where I had a sick father, an overworked mother, and no place I belonged. The Throgs Neck Branch of The New York Public Library was a converted storefront, with a children's side and an adult side. It was warm, it smelled of books and dust and lemon wax, and there was always a place for me to sit. You could take out six books on a children's card then; when you turned 13 you got an adult card, could check books out of the adult side, and could take as many as 12. I yearned to be 13.

There were storytimes at the library, but I never went to them. I would see the screen up in the corner of the children's room, and hear the rise and fall of the storyteller's voice, sometimes followed by the rising and falling of children's voices—but I never went behind the screen.

Effie Power said in her book *Library Service for Children* that the primary purpose of all storytimes is to interpret literature for children and to inspire them to read it for themselves (217). I find that a difficult point to argue with. It is, perhaps, not the only reason for storytimes, but it is definitely up there with the top three. I, however, had a different source of inspiration.

There was a librarian at the Throgs Neck Branch—a formidable woman. She was tall, black, and imposing—or maybe I found her imposing because I was none of those things. She was stern—or maybe that was because I was young. I never knew her name, but she knew mine. Looking back on it from the perspective of a youth services librarian, I realize that she had a very odd way of doing reader advisory. I would come into the library to return my books and she would say "Good afternoon, Miss Del Negro." I would mumble something completely unintelligible. She would examine the titles I had returned, and, not really looking at me, not really giving it too much visible attention, she would wave her hand toward a table in the children's room and say, "There are some books over there you might like." I always looked. And I always liked them. I had some strange idea about reading through all the fiction in alphabetical order. I made a pretty good dent in it. And then one day she came over to me and said, "I think you should look at these," and she pointed me at the 398s, the folk and fairy tales. I read them all. Eleanor Farjeon, Andrew Lang, Joseph Jacobs, Harold Courlander. After the 398s came the 292s, myths and legends—Padraic Colum, Edith Hamilton—and I was thoroughly and firmly hooked. When I found out there were actually branch libraries—what a novel idea—and that I could get to them with a bus pass, I checked out the 398s and 292s in every branch library I could get to by bus or train. That was a pretty fair number of libraries. And a pretty fair number of 398s and 292s.

Eileen Colwell once said that "the child's imagination must be stimulated from an early age if she is to develop as a person; without it she is locked into a narrow environment bounded by what she is able to see and touch" (4). In a converted storefront in the Bronx, I found not just a world, but a galaxy; not just a galaxy, but universes too numerous to count, but still close enough to touch. Years later I found myself in graduate library school, another inadvertent stumble, planning on specializing in academic libraries. I got an assistantship in the department, and met the second librarian that shaped my life. Margaret Poarch had been an army librarian before becoming a professor of children's literature. She was from the American South—two of her favorite phrases were "My country tis of thee!" and, "Honey, don't get me started." My job as Margaret's assistant consisted, among other, less important things, of pulling books for her classes. I pulled truckloads of them. And every time I did, I would say, "Gee, Margaret, I remember this book—I read it when I was a kid." After about three weeks of this, Margaret finally turned to me and said "Honey, you don't want to be an academic librarian. Academic libraries are borin'. You are a children's librarian, through and through." My fate was sealed in that tiny office in the Genesee Valley. In a way, it was very like that old library storefront—it was small, crowded, and full of books; it smelled of dust and lemon wax, and there was always someplace for me to sit, even when I had to move a stack of books off a chair in order to do it. It was Margaret who first introduced me to storytelling, and it was Margaret who told me it was the story that mattered, not the teller. "Know the story," she said. "If you know the story well enough, the rest will take care of itself. It's the story that matters, not the teller." That phrase has stayed with me all these years. It shaped the librarian, storyteller, and reviewer I was to become.

The philosophy of youth services in libraries was shaped by professional women with visionary ideals. A key element in that philosophy, a constant throughout a hundred years of public library history, was the notion that youth services in libraries existed in order to connect children to books, to the very best literature the profession could offer them. Carolyn Hewins, Anne Carroll Moore, Minerva Saunders, Effie Lee Power: we are, many of us, ignorant of their names and sometimes we forget their vision as well. Their vision included the awakening of the desire for knowledge in children who have little or no such stimulation in their personal lives; providing a connection, a bridge to powerful and beautiful literature and language; and fostering a life-long love of reading. This was both a professional and moral vison, a vision with focus and impact. Andrew Carnegie thought of the public library as the poor man's university; author Mollie Hunter once said "If you can read, you can educate yourself" (75). She also said "'If' is a little word with a very big meaning" (80).

According to the U.S. Department of Education, the percentage of illiterate adults in the United States is on the rise. Public libraries and youth services in particular lack support (if they are not under downright attack) from fiscally prudent if short-sighted private individuals and government agencies. The quest for equal access to educational opportunity for all children travels a long and tortuous route, with obstacles in the shape of monolithic bureaucracies, hostile challenges, ignorance, and greed. Any quest worthy of the name requires a heroic figure, a hero, to meet and overcome all obstacles.

The hero. That's you. Children's librarians, I mean. I've seen heroic deeds and miraculous accomplishments in the smallest storefronts. I've seen children's librarians coax non-readers into the world of books. I've seen smiling calm in the face of a roomful of adolescents bursting at the seams with an energy I only vaguely remember. I've seen libraries moved, rooms rearranged, computers installed, and new skills learned and acquired at lightning speed. I've seen quality services maintained in spite of budget and staff cuts that would cripple any corporate organization. I've seen literature-based programs created from tissue and glitter, story and song. I've seen children's rooms turned into rainforests with green construction paper and safety scissors. I've seen children's librarians stand their ground when a book is challenged, when a gang member gets belligerent, when their budget and staff are threatened.

In folktales, the hero seldom accomplishes much by herself. There is always some convenient animal helper, magical old man, or mystical wise woman to help the hero out of wells, up glass mountains, or into towers with no doors.

It's true for children's librarians as well. The best of us realize that we accomplish little on our own, that everything we do is connected to everything else. Whether we are talking about the volunteer who cuts out nametags in the thematically appropriate shape for storytime, the clerk who patiently explains for the two-hundredth time how a child gets her first library card, the page who actually displays books with attractive covers instead of the ones that just got back from the bindery—the library is a story within which all the characters are connected by blood, coincidence, or circumstance.

We Have Seen the Power

Ideally, every child you help has a supportive adult, a parent, a grandparent, a teacher, standing behind him/her. And each of those adults is a possible ally in your journey to connect children and books, children and story. They are the magical helpers in your quest to communicate the importance of children, children's books, and storytelling to the unknowing in your community. Everybody knows somebody else, and that somebody else may be the person you need to know to more effectively deliver library services to children.

And what about the child who doesn't have a supportive adult? The child who has no advocate? Well, we change roles within the story then.

We shape-shift, if you will, from hero to convenient helper. Magic man or wise woman, we are there to open the door to books and story for those children who cannot easily access what we can provide. In order to serve them effectively, it becomes necessary for us to unite with all those "everybodies" who know somebody else, to work with parents and teachers, daycare centers and preschools, health care and other community agencies.

I am familiar with the sinking feeling that providing access to literature and story for all the youth in your community is an overwheming task—the dragon is too fierce, the spell too strong, the wizard too powerful to be conquered by . . . what? A children's librarian disguised as a hero? Most of us did not become involved in children's services because it was going to be politically hazardous and fraught with difficult financial issues. Most of us became involved in children's work because we had an affinity for children, and for children's books. Ah, the books . . . "'Christmas won't be Christmas without any presents,' grumbled Jo, lying on the hearth before the fireplace" (Alcott 3). "We eat our night meal by candlelight, the four of us. Sarah has brought candles from town. And nasturtium seeds for her garden, and a book of songs for us to sing. . . . Soon there will be a wedding" (McLaughlin 58). "With a quick glance back Fox dashed toward the woods. 'The hound knows who I am!' he shouted. 'But I'm not worried. I sure can out-smart and out-run one of Mr. J.W. McCutchin's miserable mutts any old time of the day, because like I told you, I am a fox!' 'I know,' said Flossic. 'I know'" (McKissack). The books, remember? Reading as its own reward? (Oh, look, she's back on topic. . . .)

I would like to present you with a radical notion. These two affinities—our affinity for children and our affinity for children's books—are our strongest traits, the magic cloak, the seven-league boots, the water of life that will help us succeed in our quest to connect children and books, children and story.

What is it that makes the public library unique? What is it that makes us different from any other community agency? Understanding that libraries are more than books, as the professional literature is so fond of pointing out, I am standing here now to say to you that it is books that make us unique, and in the end, it is our knowledge of those books and our ability to connect them with readers that make us effective. The problem of illiteracy in the United States is no secret. We are faced with the dumbing down of everything from signage that uses symbolic pictograms to cash registers that use pictures of food instead of numbers.

How did this happen? What caused it? Who is to blame? Electronic media? Television? Computers? The Internet? As responsible adults in a responsible profession, we let it happen. And we are all to blame. We abdicated our responsibility to our clients and our collections the first time we kept silent when someone spoke denigratingly about "kiddie lit" and storytimes—"Oh, isn't that cute. You read books to children (or yourself) all day." We abdicated our responsibility the first time we said, "Oh, it doesn't matter what they read as long as they read something." We abdicated our responsibility when we decided learning a story was too much trouble, we'd show a movie instead.

Now, there's a digression waiting to happen. A century of storytelling in the library oral tradition is our heritage as youth services librarians. This heritage includes literary tales memorized with love and care; personal tales from our own lives; folktales from oral and written sources; and anything that promotes a love of language and an appreciation of the power of the written and spoken word. Many librarians started collecting, promoting, and telling traditional stories because they heard a storyteller, felt a connection to the tale and the telling, and wanted to be a part of a remarkably resilient tradition. We know that using stories with children has a number of benefits, from the practical increase of attention spans to the lyrical soaring of the soul that occurs when art is experienced. We select books and tell stories in libraries for many reasons: to build bridges between children and books, between childhood and adulthood, between language and reading, between one culture and another. In the tradition of the library professionals who have gone before us, we tell stories to keep the art of library storytelling alive.

Why do we do it? We have seen the power and authority of storytelling work its magic on the most reluctant listeners. The library literature on the promotion and use of traditional literature is based on the underlying certainty that stories will lead children to books, and that books will lead children to richer, fuller lives. Storytelling gives us heroes—not robotic transformers and metamorphosing rangers but heroes and heroines who win with wit against the powerful, with humor against the self-satisfied, and with generosity of heart against evil self-interest. Storytelling creates a community of listeners out of a group divided by age, gender, race, and economics. Promoting and telling tales from many cultures raises awareness of those cultures, and promotes pride in the cultural heritage of individual listeners. Telling tales from many cultures provides listeners with a common culture, a unity created from the diversity of many. The answer to the question "where can I find more stories?" is—books. End of digression.

We abdicated our professional responsibility when we became too involved with non-literature based programming, dog-and-pony shows for the sake of the numbers, flash and dash for the sake of a newspaper article; when we replaced storytelling with videos; when we became too busy or too tired to keep up with the literature.

Keep up with the literature. This is the pivotal issue in library services for children. You cannot effectively utilize your collection unless you know what's in it. You cannot effectively do reader advisory unless you know what is in your collection. You cannot effectively do juvenile reference unless you know what is in your collection. You cannot effectively direct other adults who work with children to the resources and materials they require unless you know your collection. You cannot effectively defend your book budget unless you know your collection. How do you know your collection? Big surprise. You read it. All of it. I know, there's no way. But try anyway. Read all the picture books. Read as much fiction as you can. Skim the non-fiction—table of contents, photos, index. You cannot defend your collection if you do not know what's in it, and you cannot know what's in it if you don't read it. Knowledge of children's literature, its history and content, is critical when formulating a collection development policy. It is also critical in giving you a sound basis for selection. No one has so much money in their book budget that they can afford to buy mediocre materials, and there is a lot of mediocrity out there. Buy multiple copies of quality, don't waste your money on mediocrity. How do you know what constitutes quality material? Read reviews, read journal articles, read the books—and then use them with children.

When people come to us, to children's librarians, they expect us to know—the books, the children, and the ways to connect them. When daycare centers, schools, and other community agencies come to us, they want the knowledge and expertise they expect professional children's librarians to have, what books work with kids, and why. Parents come in and want to know how they can help their children become readers. Teachers come in and want books for a specific curriculum unit. Homeschooolers come in and want classic titles that reflect a certain value system. Children come in and want a good book, a funny book, a mystery, or a book "like the one I read last time." You can serve them because you know the books and can talk about them in a knowledgeable fashion that inspires confidence in your selection and belief in your professional integrity.

Our second strength is our affinity for children. We like them. All of them, even the ones that drive us crazy. I always thought that what made youth service librarians so effective with children is that we are probably the only people they know who don't want anything from them. We're not their parents, so we have few expectations about their personalities or interests. We're not their teachers, so we don't pressure them about grades. We're not their coaches, so athletic prowess or lack thereof is not an issue for us. We're not their peers, so whether they are part of the right crowd is of little concern to us. We take them as they come, and as long as they are not defacing library property or engaging in obviously destructive behavior, we take them as they are. Our only concern is to connect them to the books and materials they need, the books that will help them write a paper, develop a self-concept, and formulate a world view that is bigger than their backyard, their street, their side of the road.

Children need access to libraries and information, to the knowledge and enjoyment they can provide, and we are the ones who give it to them. But despite our best intentions, it seems we are sometimes less able than we should be to communicate our place in the big picture to the community at large. How do we reach the people we need to reach in order to confirm our place in the policy-making arena? Significant, lasting change comes from the grassroots level, and grassroots change comes from networking. Being a good children's librarian gives you an instant opening with your most natural allies—the parents of the children you serve. Put up your tent and pound your drum. Every child who has a positive library and book-related experience has a message for the adults around him; every adult you convince about the importance of connecting children and books is a missionary for your cause. Push the books. Base your programming on the literature. Talk about the importance of books and reading. Turn your library into a place where reading, readers, and books are valued. Challenge your service area to become a reading community, a place where reading, readers, and books are valued. Make it a team effort. Do not waste your time on programming or events that do not promote your collection and the other resources you offer. Do literature-based programs and coordinate literature-based events that focus on the goal of creating a reading community.

GETTING THE JOB DONE

I know what you're thinking. It's too much. The hero cannot possibly sort millet seed from sand. It's too big. The giant has seven heads and the hero only one. We can't do it. One cannot carry water in a sieve.

Well, many hands make light work, the hero has a magic sword, and doing whatever is necessary to get the job done is the definition of a professional. Keep the idea of the library connecting children to books and stories at the forefront of community events. Be aware. Be responsive. Love the children, the books, the stories, your work. Know the whys and wherefores of what you do—why story times? why toddler programs? why book talks? why storytelling? why outreach? We must tell the story of the importance of connecting children and books. We must communicate the importance of positive interaction with books and print. We must communicate and nurture the spirit of discovery, the joy in story, and the intellectual curiosity that turns children into self-aware, powerful adult seekers of knowledge, on-line, off-line, and every place else.

Am I advocating a return to dusty storefronts with crowded shelves, a smell of lemon wax, and no opacs or PCs? As much as I might be sentimentally attached to the notion, I am not. I am very fond of computers. I would not give up my word processing program for love or money, and I am infinitely thrilled by *The Bulletin* Web site and the opportunities that it provides. I think cruising the information highway (remember that phrase? now relegated to yesterday's info-byte junkpile) is very handy for lots of stuff, but as a friend of mine once told me when I was learning to drive in Chicago, never get emotionally involved with traffic.

The professional literature, the journals, the newspapers, are full of articles about technology and its impact; school and public library administrators are frantically pouring hundreds of thousands of dollars into technology in a futile effort to be on the cutting edge; and computerized reading programs that give points for books read are dangerously close to becoming selection tools instead of motivational tools. We have high government officials who think we should pay kids a dollar or two for every book they read, parents who think reading certificates aren't enough of a reward for participating in the summer reading program, and school administrators who don't see the value of a well-equipped, on-site mediacenter. What's a librarian to do?

Smile. Be enthusiastic. Be informed. Pick up a book, and make them an offer they can't refuse. "In the light of the moon, a little egg lay on a leaf. One Sunday morning the warm sun came up and—pop!—out of the egg came a tiny and very hungry caterpillar" (Carle). "My great-great-great-grandmother did great things. Elizabeth lived during the Revolutionary War, but she did not fight in it" (Hearne). "The first week of August hangs at the very top of summer, the top of the live-long year, like the highest seat of a Ferris wheel when it pauses in its turning" (Babbitt 3).

Tell them a story. "Once there was and twice there wasn't," or "Most folks don't know it but the animals didn't always live on earth. Way back before 'In the beginning' and 'Once upon a time,' they lived next door to the moon" (Lester 1). Or, "When wishes were horses and beggars could ride, in a stone castle by the sea there lived a rich laird" (Del Negro), or "Once there lived a woman who had a son, a boy so round and fat, and so fond of good things to eat that everyone called him Buttercup"(Sierra and Kaminski 54).

Never underestimate the power of a story. Ruth Sawyer—one of those professional women with vision that we don't talk about nearly enough—tells in *The Way of the Storyteller* about an encounter she had with a child and a story. Sawyer was 16 and visiting Boston with her parents. She was babysitting for the seven-year-old daughter of their hosts. In the daytime all was well, but when night fell the child became frightened and uneasy until all the lamps were lit. At bedtime, she would not go to bed until Sawyer promised to stay with her and keep a light burning. Sawyer offered a story. The child resisted—she hated stories as much as she hated the dark, especially stories with witches, giants, and ogres in them. "How about fairies?" Sawyer asked. "They're elegant." Then she told the story of the boy who gathered herbs by moonlight so his mother would be healed. "It will sound better if I put out the light." She told the story three times. The next night it was the same, and the next, until "dark came gently, with it the stars, the call of the screech owl, and all the little sounds of earth that came with spring. Together we felt the comfortable darkness fold us in." Years later Sawyer met the young girl in a cafeteria. Each was unsure of the other's identity at first, until the girl, now an eighth-grader, cried out: "I know who you are! You're the girl who made me like the dark" (Sawyer 83-84).

I think sometimes we have lost our focus, our sense of our profession's history and philosophy. It helps to return to that basic but irreplaceable premise: the right book for the right child at the right time. It helps to develop something of an attitude, as well. My friend Michael, a former children's librarian, had it down cold. When asked by a well-meaning but apparently uninformed parent what the reward was for reading a book in the summer reading program, Michael, a most elegant dresser, would let his reading glasses slide down to the end of his nose, peer disdainfully over them, and reply precisely and succinctly: "Madam, reading is its own reward."

Ruth Sawyer would have approved.

WORKS CITED

Alcott, Louisa May. *Little Women*. New York: Crowell, 1955.
Babbitt, Natalie. *Tuck Everlasting*. New York: Farrar, Straus, Giroux, 1975.
Blake, William. "The Tyger." *Songs of Innocence and Experience: Shewing the Two Contrary States of the Human Soul 1789-1794*. London: Oxford U P, 1977. Pl. 42.
Carle, Eric. *The Very Hungry Caterpillar*. New York: Philomel, 1969.
Cowell, Eileen. *Storytelling*. London: Bodley Head, 1980.
Del Negro, Janice M. *Lucy Dove*. New York: DK Ink, 1998.
Hearne, Betsy. *Seven Brave Women*. New York: Greenwillow, 1997.
Hood, Thomas. "Bridge of Sighs." *The Golden Treasury: Selected from the Best Songs and Lyrical Poems in the English Language*. Ed. Francis Palgrave. Rev. ed. New York: MacMillan, 1966.
Hunter, Mollie. *The Pied Piper Syndrome, and Other Essays*. New York: HarperCollins, 1992.
Lester, Julius. *The Tales of Uncle Remus: The Adventures of Brer Rabbit*. New York: Dial, 1987.
MacLachlan, Patricia. *Sarah, Plain and Tall*. New York: Harper & Row, 1985.
McKissack, Patricia C. *Flossie and the Fox*. New York: Dial, 1986.
Power, Effie L. *Library Service for Children*. Chicago: ALA, 1930.
Sawyer, Ruth. *The Way of the Storyteller*. New York: Viking, 1942.
Scott, Sir Walter. "Marmion." *The Complete Poetical Works of Sir Walter Scott*. Boston: Houghton Mifflin, 1900. 130.
Sierra, Judy and Robert Kaminski. *Twice Upon a Time: Stories to Tell, Retell, Act Out and Write About*. Bronx: H. W. Wilson, 1989.
Speare, Morris Edmund. *The Pocket Book of Verse: Great English and American Poems*. New York: Pocket Books, 1940.
United States Department of Education, National Center for Educational Statistics. *1992 National Adult Literacy Survey*. 23 June 1998. <http://nces.ed.gov/nadlits/trends.html>.

Concluding Our Story of Stories

The final session of "Story: From Fireplace to Cyberspace" ended late on a sunny Tuesday morning with one last song and story from Joseph Sobol, and Janice Del Negro's welcome words to attendees, "Go forth. Eat lunch. Tell stories." And so they did. And so we have, in editing and shaping these proceedings, which is the story of stories from fireplace to cyberspace.

To some, stories and storytelling belong to a distant time of stone knives and petroglyphs. Hunter-gatherers had stories. Primitive societies had stories. And storytelling requires a wood fire and a dark night. But of course stories may be found not only at the family dinner table or with the last survivor of the Titanic. Stories are also in the next booth at a fast food restaurant, in the bleachers during the seventh-inning stretch, and in the classrooms (and in the teachers' lounge) of an elementary school. Stories may even be heard while standing in the ticket line for the latest Disney animated feature. In our interest in child welfare, we often forget that children are not simply passive receptacles for whatever treasure or trash the adult world throws at them, but are lively agents who are continually interacting with their environment. Children actively create meaning as readers, viewers, and listeners. And so, of course, do adults. To use one more technological image, stories appear to be hardwired into the human psyche.

The traditional oral narrative, which reaches only those within the range of the storyteller's voice, can seem like an endangered species in the media-rich (and often content-poor) environment of contemporary U.S. society. The reverence we feel for traditional stories can cause us to try to preserve them just as they are, unchanged, a precious treasure to be kept secluded from the hustle and bustle of life in a technologically advanced society that seems to worship the newest trend, the latest gizmo, the densest hard drive and the most capacious memory. This enshrinement, however, can become a mindless dogmatism in the cause of the real Cinderella, the true Jack and the Beanstalk, the original Anansi that ignores the enduring and fluid nature of stories themselves.

Paradoxically, stories are both as fragile as orchids and as hearty as dandelions. They call forth our protective urges, yet they spring up like the weeds we strive to eradicate. Stories endure and adapt and grow and flourish. Stories survive.

CJ

ANNE SHIMOJIMA
School Library Media Specialist/IMC Teacher
Braeside School
Highland Park, Illinois

Appendix A
Storytelling in the School Library Media Center: Bibliography and Resources

STORY BIBLIOGRAPHY

Bang, Molly. *Wiley and the Hairy Man.* New York: Macmillan, 1976.

Chase, Richard, ed. "Old Fire Dragaman." *The Jack Tales.* Boston: Houghton, 1943. 106-13.

—, ed. "Like Meat Loves Salt." *Grandfather Tales: American-English Folk Tales.* Boston: Houghton, 1948. 124-28.

—, ed. "Soap, Soap, Soap." *Grandfather Tales: American-English Folk Tales.* Boston: Houghton, 1948. 130-35.

Hardendorff, Jeanne. *Slip! Slop! Gobble!* Philadelphia: Lippincott, 1970.

Jacobs, Joseph. "Mr. Fox." *English Folk and Fairy Tales.* New York: Putnam, n.d. 153-58.

Kimmel, Eric. *The Three Sacks of Truth: A Story from France.* New York: Holiday House, 1993.

Leodhas, Sorche Nic. "Twelve Great Black Cats and the Red One." *Twelve Black Cats, and Other Eerie Scottish Tales.* New York: Dutton, 1971. 3-11.

BOOKS ABOUT STORIES AND STORYTELLING: AN ANNOTATED LIST

Barton, Bob. *Stories in the Classroom: Storytelling, Reading Aloud and Roleplaying with Children.* Portsmouth: Heinemann, 1990.

> This inspiring book about the importance of "storying" with children interweaves storytelling and reading aloud. Many suggestions are given on helping students respond to stories.

—. *Tell Me Another: Storytelling and Reading Aloud at Home, at School, and in the Community.* Portsmouth: Heinemann, 1986.

> Covers both storytelling and reading aloud with advice on how to select a story and make it your own. Includes activities for the classroom such as call and response stories, sound exploration, chanting, drama games, story theater, and round-robin storytelling.

Bauer, Caroline Feller. *Caroline Feller Bauer's New Handbook for Storytellers: With Stories, Poems, Magic, and More.* Chicago: American Library Association, 1993.

>Here is a wealth of suggestions on how to tell stories, including multimedia storytelling with music, puppets, flip cards, objects, flannel, felt, and magnetic boards, slides, filmstrips, film, and video. Includes a bibliography of stories by subject.

Bettelheim, Bruno. *The Uses of Enchantment: The Meaning and Importance of Fairy Tales.* New York: Knopf, 1976.

>Bettleheim's explanation of how and why fairy tales help children to understand themselves and their world, create meaning in their lives, and build an inner sense of security.

Birch, Carol L. and Melissa A. Heckler, eds. *Who Says? Essays in Pivotal Issues on Contemporary Storytelling.* Little Rock: August House, 1996.

>Ten thoughtful and insightful essays comment on such issues as the storyteller as narrator, playing with the "fourth wall," misconceptions about folktales, Jewish models of storytelling, Native American storytelling, and the reciprocity between the teller and the listener.

Breneman, Lucille and Bren Breneman. *Once Upon a Time: A Storytelling Handbook.* Chicago: Nelson-Hall, 1983.

>Detailed guidance on storytelling: selecting a story, analyzing and adapting a story, achieving fluency, working with characters, working for visualization, body control, and polish. One chapter focuses on story biography. Includes an annotated bibliography of stories good for telling.

Bruchac, Joseph. *Tell Me a Tale: A Book About Storytelling.* San Diego: Harcourt Brace, 1997.

>Aimed at younger readers, this book takes readers through the four cornerstones of storytelling: listening, observing, remembering, and sharing. Includes 14 stories from around the world and Bruchac's Native American background.

Chinen, Allan B. *In the Ever After: Fairy Tales and the Second Half of Life.* Wilmette: Chiron Publications, 1989.

>A thoughtful and insightful book that looks at the psychological tasks of the mature adult and examines 15 elder tales which depict these tasks symbolically.

—. *Once Upon a Midlife: Classic Stories and Mythic Tales to Illuminate the Middle Years.* New York: Putnam's, 1992.

>A collection of 16 stories chosen for their ability to pinpoint the issues of midlife, along with commentaries drawn from Dr. Chinen's clinical experience and literature from around the world.

Collins, Rives and Pamela Cooper. *The Power of Story: Teaching Through Storytelling.* 2nd ed. Scottsdale: Gorsuch Scarisbrick, 1997.

> Excellent resource that covers the hows and whys of storytelling and also includes a chapter on story dramatization and lots of activities to use when teaching children storytelling.

Dailey, Sheila. *Putting the World in a Nutshell: The Art of the Formula Tale.* Bronx: H. W. Wilson, 1994.

> Nine basic types of formula tales—chain, cumulative, circle, endless, catch, compound triad, question, air castles, and good/bad—are examined and 38 stories are included.

De Vos, Gail. *Storytelling for Young Adults: Techniques and Treasury.* Englewood: Libraries Unlimited, 1991.

> Excellent resource that discusses the value of telling to young adults (ages 13-18), reviews storytelling techniques, describes extensions in the classroom, and includes an annotated bibliography of about 250 stories arranged by genre: folktales and fairy tales; myths and legends; ghost, horror, and suspense stories; urban belief legends; love and romance stories; twists, satire, and exaggeration stories; and literary stories.

De Wit, Dorothy. *Children's Faces Looking Up: Program Building for the Storyteller.* Chicago: American Library Association, 1979.

> The first half of the book is an excellent background in story selection, sources, modifying stories, and tips for tellers. The second half gives six sample story programs with such themes as food, animal stories, magic, shoes and feet, journeys, and color.

Gillard, Marni. *Storyteller, Storyteacher: Discovering the Power of Storytelling for Teaching and Living.* York: Stenhouse, 1996.

> Gillard describes how she brought storytelling into the lives and lessons of her middle school students, but what she has learned about stories, storying, and storytelling in her life will speak to students and teachers of all ages.

Greene, Ellin. *Storytelling: Art and Technique.* 3rd. ed. New Providence: R. R. Bowker, 1996.

> An excellent and practical introduction to storytelling with some emphasis on librarians planning story programs. Includes chapters on children as storytellers, telling to young adults, special settings and needs, and lists of stories by age. Thirteen stories are included.

Holt, David and Bill Mooney, eds. *The Storyteller's Guide: Storytellers Share Advice for the Classroom, Boardroom, Showroom, Podium, Pulpit, and Center Stage.* Little Rock: August House, 1996.

> More than 50 of the country's leading storytellers answer such questions as: How do I get started? How do I find the right stories? How

do I shape stories from the printed text? What performance techniques do I need to know? What mistakes are frequently made by beginning storytellers? What are the ethics of storytelling? How do I market myself? What is the life of a professional storyteller like? How can a teacher use storytelling in the classroom? How can a media specialist improve and expand storytelling in the library? What was your worst storytelling experience? Insight, practical guidance, and humor in an extremely valuable guide.

Livo, Norma J. and Sandra A. Rietz. *Storytelling: Process and Practice.* Littleton: Libraries Unlimited, 1986.

A very complete resource that explains the function of storytelling; how to develop story memory; how to prepare, develop, and deliver stories; and how to work with audiences. Includes an excellent discussion of story structure and integrated units around the themes of frogs and rainbows.

—. *Storytelling Activities.* Littleton: Libraries Unlimited, 1987.

A book of activities for storytellers and/or children to aid in finding, designing, presenting, and delivering stories. Ties each activity to Bloom's Taxonomy and a scale of educational skills.

MacDonald, Margaret Read. *The Storyteller's Start-Up Book: Finding, Learning, Performing, and Using Folktales Including Twelve Tellable Tales.* Little Rock: August House, 1993.

Insightful guidance on how to get started telling stories, including how to look at stories critically and accepting the role of the storyteller. Extremely helpful bibliographies broken down by theme.

Maguire, Jack. *Creative Storytelling: Choosing, Inventing, and Sharing Tales for Children.* New York: McGraw-Hill, 1985.

Includes helpful chapters on the history of storytelling, various types of stories, and creating your own stories.

McAdams, Dan P. *Stories We Live By: Personal Myths and the Making of the Self.* New York: W. Morrow, 1993.

A theory of human identity that explains how we make sense of our lives by structuring our life episodes into the stories we tell about ourselves, creating a personal myth.

Mellon, Nancy. *Storytelling and the Art of Imagination.* Rockport: Element, Inc., 1992.

A guidebook to the symbolic elements of stories: beginnings, endings, movement, direction, natural elements of the earth, journeys, seasons, moods, story characters, and power symbols.

Moore, Robin. *Awakening the Hidden Storyteller: How to Build a Storytelling Tradition in Your Family.* Boston: Shambhala, 1991.

Tips on telling stories with a look at the inner processes: voyaging through time, finding your voice, exploring the landscape of the imagination.

National Storytelling Association. *Many Voices: True Tales from America's Past.* Jonesborough: National Storytelling Press, 1995.

Thirty-six stories that put a human face onto American history, from 1643 to the present, told by the storytellers of today. Also available: National Storytelling Association. *Many Voices: Teacher's Guide.* Jonesborough: National Storytelling Press, 1995.

—. *Tales as Tools: The Power of Story in the Classroom.* Jonesborough: National Storytelling Press, 1994.

An outstanding resource on how to use storytelling to teach reading, writing, peace, the environment, history, science, math; to build community; and to heal.

Pellowski, Anne. *The World of Storytelling.* Exp. and rev. ed. Bronx: H. W. Wilson, 1990.

A scholarly work describing storytelling traditions throughout the world and through history, including bardic, religious, folk, theatrical, library, institutional, and therapeutic storytelling. Also described are various styles, openings and closings, musical accompaniment, pictures and objects, and training of storytellers. An extensive bibliography is included.

Rosen, Betty. *And None of It Was Nonsense: The Power of Storytelling in School.* Portsmouth: Heinemann, 1988.

Rosen describes how she used storytelling, including Greek mythology, with groups of multicultural, multilanguage boys from 8 to18 in an English school.

Ross, Ramon. *Storyteller: The Classic that Heralded America's Storytelling Revival.* 3rd rev. ed. Little Rock: August House, 1996.

A thoughtful treatment of storytelling. Includes chapters on choral reading, flannel boards, puppets, singing and dancing, and reading aloud.

Sawyer, Ruth. *The Way of the Storyteller.* New York: Viking, 1962.

First published in 1942, this chronicle of Sawyer's own development as a storyteller offers practical suggestions and insights along with 11 of her stories.

Schimmel, Nancy. *Just Enough to Make a Story: A Sourcebook for Storytelling.* 3rd ed. Berkeley: Sister's Choice Press,1992.

Concise, clear, and very helpful. Gives many resources including lists of stories of active heroines, stories for peace, ecological stories, and stories for adults.

Shedlock, Marie L. *The Art of the Story-Teller.* 3rd ed. New York: Dover, 1951.

> First published in 1915, the thoughts and advice of a master storyteller who gave inspiration to the beginnings of the library storytelling tradition in the U.S. Includes 18 stories.

Smith, Charles A. *From Wonder to Wisdom: Using Stories to Help Children Grow.* New York: New American Library, 1989.

> Summarizes the eight themes in stories that affect a child's self-worth: becoming a goal seeker, confronting challenges courageously, growing closer to others, coming to terms with loss, offering kindness to others, preserving an openness to the world, becoming a social problem-solver, and forming a positive self-image; and suggests books/stories for each theme.

Trousdale, Ann M. *Give a Listen: Stories of Storytelling in School.* Urbana: National Council of Teachers of English, 1994.

> Teachers in all grades tell how storytelling creates classrooms of listeners and learners.

Yolen, Jane. *Touch Magic: Fantasy, Faerie and Folklore in the Literature of Childhood.* New York: Philomel, 1981.

> Insightful essays about the importance of fairy tales and fantasy in nourishing our humanity.

Zipes, Jack. *Creative Storytelling: Building Community, Changing Lives.* New York: Routledge, 1995.

> Zipes, an expert on fairy tales and children's literature, shares his ideas on the use of storytelling with children. Creative activities are described that emphasize social issues and respect for children.

BOOKS ABOUT FAMILY STORYTELLING

Akeret, Robert. *Family Tales, Family Wisdom: How to Gather the Stories of a Lifetime and Share Them with Your Family.* New York: Morrow, 1991.

Collins, Chase. *Tell Me a Story: Creating Bedtime Tales Your Children Will Dream On.* Boston: Houghton, 1992.

Davis, Donald. *Telling Your Own Stories: For Family and Classroom Storytelling, Public Speaking, and Personal Journaling.* Little Rock: August House, 1993.

Fletcher, William. *Recording Your Family History: A Guide to Preserving Oral History with Videotape, Audiotape, Suggested Topics and Questions, Interview Techniques.* New York: Dodd, Mead & Company, 1986.

Greene, Bob and D. G. Fulford. *To Our Children's Children: Preserving Family Histories for Generations to Come.* New York: Doubleday, 1993.

Pellowski, Anne. *The Family Storytelling Handbook: How to Use Stories, Anecdotes, Rhymes, Handkerchiefs, Paper, and Other Objects to Enrich Your Family Traditions.* New York: Macmillan, 1987.

Stone, Elizabeth. *Black Sheep and Kissing Cousins: How Our Family Stories Shape Us.* New York: Penguin, 1989.

Weitzman, David. *My Backyard History Book.* Boston: Little, Brown & Company, 1975.

Zeitlin, Steven J. *A Celebration of American Family Folklore: Tales and Traditions from the Smithsonian Collection.* New York: Pantheon, 1982.

BOOKS ABOUT TEACHING STORYTELLING TO CHILDREN

Hamilton, Martha. *Children Tell Stories: A Teaching Guide.* Katonah: Richard C. Owen Publishers, 1990.

Kinghorn, Harriet R. *Every Child a Storyteller: A Handbook of Ideas.* Englewood: Teacher Ideas Press, 1991.

Lipman, Doug. *Storytelling Games: Creative Activities for Language, Communication, and Composition Across the Curriculum.* Phoenix: Oryx Press, 1995.

Pellowski, Anne. *The Storytelling Handbook: A Young People's Collection of Unusual Tales and Helpful Hints on How to Tell Them.* New York: Simon & Schuster Books for Young Readers, 1995.

BOOKS ABOUT URBAN LEGENDS

Brunvand, Jan Harold. *The Choking Doberman and Other "New" Urban Legends.* New York: W.W. Norton, 1984.

—. *The Mexican Pet: More "New" Urban Legends and Some Old Favorites.* New York: W.W. Norton, 1986.

—. *The Vanishing Hitchhiker: American Urban Legends and Their Meaning.* New York: W.W. Norton, 1981.

GENERAL STORY COLLECTIONS

Brody, Ed, ed. *Spinning Tales, Weaving Hope: Stories of Peace, Justice, and the Environment.* Philadelphia: New Society Publishers, 1992.

Caduto, Michael J. and Joseph Bruchac. *Keepers of the Earth: Native American Stories and Environmental Activities for Children.* Golden: Fulcrum, 1988.

Cole, Joanna and Jill K. Schwarz, eds. *Best-Loved Folktales of the World.* Garden City: Anchor-Doubleday, 1982.

Davis, Donald. *Jack Always Seeks His Fortune: Authentic Appalachian Jack Tales.* Little Rock: August House, 1992.

DeSpain, Pleasant. *Thirty-Three Multicultural Tales to Tell.* Little Rock: August House, 1993.

Goss, Linda and Marian E. Barnes, eds. *Talk That Talk: An Anthology of African-American Storytelling.* New York: Simon & Schuster, 1989.

Haley, Gail E. *Mountain Jack Tales.* New York: Dutton Children's Books, 1992.

Hearne, Betsy. *Beauties and Beasts.* Phoenix: Oryx, 1993.

Holt, David and Bill Mooney, eds. *Ready-To-Tell Tales.* Little Rock: August House, 1994.

MacDonald, Margaret Read. *Peace Tales: World Folktales to Talk About.* Hamden: Linnet Books, 1992.

—. *Twenty Tellable Tales: Audience Participation Folktales for the Beginning Storyteller.* New York: Wilson, 1986.

—. *When the Lights Go Out: Twenty Scary Tales to Tell.* Bronx: H. W. Wilson, 1988.

Miller, Teresa. *Joining In: An Anthology of Audience Participation Stories & How to Tell Them.* Cambridge: Yellow Moon Press, 1988.

The National Association for the Preservation and Perpetuation of Storytelling. *Best-Loved Stories Told at the National Storytelling Festival.* Jonesborough: National Storytelling Press, 1991.

—. *More Best-Loved Stories Told at the National Storytelling Festival.* Jonesborough: National Storytelling Press, 1992.

Pellowski, Anne. *Hidden Stories in Plant: Unusual and Easy-to-Tell Stories from Around the World Together with Creative Things to Do While Telling Them.* New York: Macmillan, 1990.

—. *The Story Vine: A Source Book of Unusual and Easy-to-Tell Stories from Around the World.* New York: Macmillan, 1984.

Shannon, George, comp. *A Knock at the Door.* Phoenix: Oryx Press, 1992.

Sierra, Judy, ed. *Cinderella.* Phoenix: Oryx Press, 1992.

Sierra, Judy and Robert Kaminski. *Twice Upon a Time: Stories to Tell, Retell, Act Out, and Write About.* Bronx: H.W. Wilson, 1989.

Smith, Jimmy Neil, ed. *Homespun: Tales from America's Favorite Storytellers.* New York: Crown, 1988.

Yolen, Jane, ed. *Favorite Folktales From Around the World.* New York: Pantheon, 1986.

INDEXES AND REFERENCES

Ashliman, D. L. *A Guide to Folktales in the English Language: Based on the Aarne-Thompson Classification System.* New York: Greenwood Press, 1987.

Eastman, Mary. *Index to Fairy Tales, Myths, and Legends.* Boston: F. W. Faxon, 1926. Also *Index to Fairy Tales, Myths, and Legends.* Supplement. F. W. Faxon: Boston, 1937; and *Index to Fairy Tales, Myths, and Legends.* 2nd Supplement. F. W. Faxon: Boston, 1952.

Ireland, Norma. *Index to Fairy Tales, 1949-1972: Including Folklore, Legends, and Myths in Collections.* Westwood: F. W. Faxon, 1973.

Lima, Carolyn W. and John A. Lima. *A to Zoo: Subject Access to Children's Picture Books.* 4th ed. New Providence: R.R. Bowker, 1993.

MacDonald, Margaret Read. *The Storyteller's Sourcebook.: A Subject, Title and Motif Index to Folklore Collections for Children.* Detroit: Neal-Schuman Publishers—Gale Research, 1982.

Periodicals

National Association of Black Storytellers Newsletter
P.O. Box 67722
Baltimore, MD 21215

Parabola Magazine: Myth and Tradition and the Search for Meaning
Society for the Study of Myth and Tradition
656 Broadway
New York, NY 10012

Jewish Storytelling Newsletter
92nd St. YM-YWHA Library
1395 Lexington Ave.
New York, NY 10128

Storytelling Magazine
National Storytelling Association
P.O. Box 309
Jonesborough, TN 37659

Storytelling World
Dr. Flora Joy
East Tennessee State University
Box 70647
Johnson City, TX 37614-0647

Organizations and Events

The Illinois Storytelling Festival is held in Spring Grove, Illinois, every year during the last weekend in July. This outdoor festival features workshops, a late-night ghost story program, hourly story sessions, and spiritual stories.

Illinois Storytelling Festival
P.O. Box 507
Richmond, IL 60071
(815) 344-0181

NSA sponsors the National Storytelling Festival, held every October in Jonesborough, Tennessee, and various workshops and conferences around the country. It publishes *Storytelling Magazine* and *The National Storytelling Directory*, which lists storytellers, festivals, conferences, centers, organizations and guilds, newsletters, and educational opportunities ($7.95, free to NSA members). NSA also sells books, cassettes, and videos (call 1-800-525-4514 to order, or for a brochure).

National Storytelling Association (NSA)
(Formerly National Association for the Preservation and Perpetuation of Storytelling, NAPPS)
P.O. Box 309
Jonesborough, TN 37659
(800) 525-4514

S TORYTELLING R ESOURCES ON THE I NTERNET
The Children's Literature Web. Ed. David K. Brown. 1 June 1998. <http://www.ucalgary.ca/~dkbrown/index.html>.
The Encyclopedia Mythica. Ed. M. F. Lindemans. 1 June 1998. <http://www.pantheon.org/mythica/>. An encyclopedia on myth, folklore, and legend.
Illinois Storytelling Festival. 29 June 1998. <http://www.storytelling.org/>.
McWilliams, Barry. *The Art of Storytelling.* 1 June 1998. <http://kirov.seanet.com/~eldrbarry/roos/art.htm>.
Myths and Legends. Ed. Christopher B. Siren. <http://pubpages.unh.edu/~cbsiren/myth.html>.
National Storytelling Association. Home page. 1 June 1998. <http://www.storynet.org>. The website of the NSA includes a searchable directory of 600 storytellers plus information on 200 organizations, 200 events, 100 educational opportunities, The National Storytelling Center, The National Storytelling Conference, and Jonesborough, Tennessee, site of the National Storytelling Festival.
Northern Appalachian Storytelling Festival. Ed. Mike Leiboff. <http://wso.net/storyfest/>. Includes interviews with storytellers.
Storyteller Net. Ed. Michael T. Abrams. 29 June 1998. <http://www.storyteller.net>
Storytelling FAQ. Ed. Tim Sheppard. 1 June 1998. <http://www.lilliput.co.uk/faq.html>.

STORYTELL—This listserv provides a lively discussion on storytelling issues. When you subscribe, any message sent by any member is e-mailed to your mailbox.

To subscribe:
 1. Send an e-mail message to: listserv@venus.twu.edu
 2. Leave the subject line blank
 3. In the message area write: subscribe storytell

To go to the STORYTELL archives, searchable by keyword: *Archives of TWU Discussion Lists.* Texas Woman's University. 1 June 1998. <http://www.twu.edu/lists/>.

Cinderella Variants

Ceylon—Tooze, Ruth. "A Girl and a Stepmother." *The Wonderful Wooden Peacock Flying Machine and Other Tales of Ceylon.* New York: Day, 1969. 50-54.

China— Hume, Lotta. "A Chinese Cinderella." *Favorite Children's Stories From China and Tibet.* Tokyo: Tuttle, 1962. 15-22.

    Louie, Ai-Ling. *Yeh-Shen: A Cinderella Story from China.* New York: Philomel, 1982.

Egypt—Climo, Shirley. *The Egyptian Cinderella.* New York: Crowell, 1989.

England—Jacobs, Joseph. "Rushen Coatie." *More English Fairy Tales.* New York: Putnam's, n.d. 163-68.

—. "Tattercoats." *More English Fairy Tales.* New York: Putnam's, n.d. 67-72.

Europe—Jacobs, Joseph. "The Cinder-Maid." *European Folk and Fairy Tales.* New York: Putnam's, 1916. 1-12.

    Huck, Charlotte. *Princess Furball.* New York: Greenwillow, 1989.

Finland—Bowman, James C. and Margery Bianco. "Liisa and the Prince." *Tales from a Finnish Tupa.* Trans. Aili Kolehmainen. Chicago: Whitman, 1950. 187-198.

France—Galdone, Paul. *Cinderella.* New York: McGraw-Hill, 1978.

    Perrault, Charles. *The Complete Fairy Tales of Charles Perrault.* New York: Clarion, 1993.

Germany—Crane, Lucy, trans. "Aschenputtel." *Household Stories from the Collection of the Brothers Grimm.* New York: McGraw-Hill, 1966. 118-25.

Iceland—Sperry, Margaret. "The Golden Shoe." *Scandinavian Stories.* New York: F. Watts, 1971. 277-88.

Ireland—Jacobs, Joseph. "Fair, Brown, and Trembling." *Celtic Fairy Tales.* New York: Putnam's, n.d. 184-97.

Italy—Haviland, Virginia. "Cenerentola." *Favorite Fairy Tales Told in Italy.* Boston: Little, Brown, 1965. 3-18.

Japan—Seki, Keigo, ed. "Benizara and Kakezara." *Folktales of Japan.* Chicago: University of Chicago Press, 1963. 120-34.

Korea—Climo, Shirley. *The Korean Cinderella.* New York: HarperCollins, 1993.

Native American—Arbuthnot, May Hill. "Little Burnt Face." *Time for Old Magic.* Chicago: Scott, Foresman, 1970. 258-61.

    Martin, Rafe. *The Rough-Face Girl.* New York: Putnam's, 1992.

    San Souci, Robert D. *Sootface: An Ojibwa Cinderella Story.* New York: Doubleday Books for Young Readers, 1994.

Serbia—Spicer, Dorothy. "The Enchanted Cow." *Long Ago in Serbia.* Philadelphia: Westminster, 1968. 47-69.

U.S.A.—Chase, Richard, ed. "Ashpet." *Grandfather Tales: American-English Folk Tales.* Boston: Houghton, 1948. 115-23.

APPENDIX A/SCHOOL LIBRARY MEDIA CENTER 119

—, ed. "Catskins." *Grandfather Tales: American-English Folk Tales.* Boston: Houghton, 1948. 106-14.

Compton, Joanne. *Ashpet: An Appalachian Tale.* New York: HolidayHouse, 1994.

Hooks, William. *Moss Gown.* New York: Clarion, 1987.

Vietnam—Graham, Gail. "The Jeweled Slipper." *The Beggar in the Blanket and Other Vietnamese Tales.* New York: Dial, 1970. 11-21.

Vuong, Lynette Dyer. "The Brocaded Slipper." *The Brocaded Slipper and Other Vietnamese Tales.* Reading: Addison-Wesley, 1982. 1-26.

Modern-day and Animal Versions—Jackson, Ellen. *Cinder Edna.* New York: Lothrop, Lee & Shepard, 1994.

Minters, Frances. *Cinder-Elly.* New York: Viking, 1994.

Myers, Bernice. *Sidney Rella and the Glass Sneaker.* New York: Macmillan, 1985.

Perlman, Janet. *Cinderella Penguin, or, The Little Glass Flipper.* New York: Viking, 1993.

Collection—Sierra, Judy. *Cinderella.* Phoenix: Oryx Press, 1992. Contains 25 Cinderella variations from around the world.

STORIES ABOUT JACK

Chase, Richard, ed. *Grandfather Tales: American-English Folk Tales.* Boston: Houghton, 1948.

—, ed. *The Jack Tales.* Boston: Houghton, 1943.

Compton, Kenn and Joanne Compton. *Jack the Giant Chaser: An Appalachian Tale.* New York: Holiday House, 1993.

Davis, Donald. *Jack Always Seeks His Fortune: Authentic Appalachian Jack Tales.* Little Rock: August House, 1992.

—. *Jack and the Animals: An Appalachian Folktale.* Little Rock: August House, 1995.

Haley, Gail. *Jack and the Fire Dragon.* New York: Crown, 1988.

—. *Mountain Jack Tales.* New York: Dutton, 1992.

McCarthy, William Bernard. *Jack in Two Worlds: Contemporary North American Tales and Their Tellers.* Chapel Hill: The University of North Carolina Press, 1994.

STORIES TO REWRITE

Bruchac, Joseph. *The First Strawberries: A Cherokee Story.* New York: Dial Books for Young Readers, 1993.

Chase, Richard, ed. "Old One-Eye." *The Grandfather Tales: American-English Folk Tales.* Boston: Houghton, 1948. 205-07.

Demi. *The Empty Pot.* New York: Henry Holt, 1990.

Grimm, Jacob. "The Hare and the Hedgehog." *The Complete Grimm's Fairy Tales.* New York: Pantheon, 1972. 760-64.

Hong, Lily Toy. *How Ox Star Fell from Heaven.* Morton Grove: Albert Whitman, 1991.
—. *Two of Everything: A Chinese Folk Tale.* Morton Grove: Albert Whitman, 1992.
Montgomerie, Norah. "The Gold Dust that Turned to Sand." *Twenty-Five Fables.* London: Abelard-Schuman, 1961. 58-59.
—. "The Monkey and the Shark." *Twenty-Five Fables.* London: Abelard-Schuman, 1961. 26-27.
Schwartz, Howard. "Moving a Mountain." *The Diamond Tree: Jewish Tales from Around the World.* New York: HarperCollins, 1991. 85-92.
Simms, Laura. "A Single Grain of Rice." *Stories Old as the World, Fresh as the Rain.* Weston: Weston Woods, WW-712, 1981.
Singer, Isaac. "The Snow in Chelm." *Zlateh the Goat, and Other Stories.* New York: HarperCollins, 1966. 29-34.
Wyndham, Lee. "How the Sons Filled the Hut." *Tales the People Tell in Russia.* New York: J. Messner, 1970. 13-15.

A GOOD STORY FOR CHILDREN TO WRITE AN ENDING
Credle, Ellis. "The Pudding that Broke up the Preaching." *Tall Tales from the High Hills, and Other Stories.* New York: T. Nelson, 1957. 21-26.

STORYTELLING AND CREATIVE DRAMA
Chase, Richard, ed. "Sody Salleratus." *Grandfather Tales: American-English Folk Tales.* Boston: Houghton, 1948. 75-79.
Chinen, Allan. "The Man with the Bump." *In the Ever After: Fairy Tales and the Second Half of Life.* Wilmette: Chiron Publications, 1989. 75-78.
DeSpain, Pleasant. "The Extraordinary Cat." *Twenty-Two Splendid Tales to Tell from Around the World, Vol. 2.* 3rd ed. Little Rock: August House, 1994. (A variation of this story is Kimmel, Eric. *The Greatest of All: A Japanese Folktale.* Little Rock: Holiday House, 1991.)
Flack, Marjorie. *Ask Mr. Bear.* New York: Macmillan, 1932.
Galdone, Paul. *Henny Penny.* New York: Seabury, 1968.
—. *The Greedy Old Fat Man.* New York: Clarion, 1983.
Simms, Laura. *The Squeaky Door.* New York: Crown, 1990.
Tolstoy, Aleksey. *The Great Big Enormous Turnip.* New York: F. Watts, 1968.

FOLKTALE UNIT: SECOND GRADE
• Read Aloud/Tell—Fairy Tales
Read:
Rogasky, Barbara. *The Water of Life: A Tale from the Brothers Grimm.* New York: Holiday House, 1986.
Tell:
Mayer, Marianna. *The Twelve Dancing Princesses.* New York: William Morrow, 1989.

Jacob Grimm and Wilhelm Grimm. "Goose Girl." *The Complete Grimm's Fairy Tales.* New York: Pantheon, 1972. 404-11.
—. "King Thrushbeard." *The Complete Grimm's Fairy Tales.* New York: Pantheon, 1972. 244-48.
—. "Little Briar Rose." *The Complete Grimm's Fairy Tales.* New York: Pantheon, 1972. 237-41.
—. "Mother Holle." *The Complete Grimm's Fairy Tales.* New York: Pantheon, 1972. 133-36.
—. "One-Eye, Two-Eyes, Three-Eyes." *The Complete Grimm's Fairy Tales.* New York: Pantheon, 1972. 585-92.
—. "The Queen Bee." *The Complete Grimm's Fairy Tales.* New York: Pantheon, 1972. 317-19.
—. "Rapunzel." *The Complete Grimm's Fairy Tales.* New York: Pantheon, 1972. 73-77.
—. "The Six Swans." *The Complete Grimm's Fairy Tales.* New York: Pantheon, 1972. 232-37.

• Read Aloud/Tell—Cinderella Variations
Tell:
Egypt—Climo, Shirley. *The Egyptian Cinderella.* New York: Crowell, 1989.
Germany—Grimm, Jacob and Wilhelm Grimm. "Cinderella." *The Complete Grimm's Fairy Tales.* New York: Pantheon, 1972. 121-28.
Korea—Climo, Shirley. *The Korean Cinderella.* New York: HarperCollins, 1993.
Native American—Martin, Rafe. *The Rough-Face Girl.* New York: Putnam's, 1992.
U.S.A.—Compton, Joanne. *Ashpet: An Appalachian Tale.* New York: Holiday House, 1994.

• Read Aloud—Folktales
Africa—Paterson, Katherine. *The Tale of the Mandarin Ducks.* New York: Lodestar, 1990.
Europe—DePaola, Tomie. *Fin M'Coul: The Giant of Knockmany Hill.* New York: Holiday House, 1981.
South America—Flora. *Feathers Like a Rainbow: An Amazon Indian Tale.* New York: Harper & Row, 1989.
North America—Stevens, Janet. *Tops and Bottoms.* San Diego: Harcourt Brace, 1995.

• Storytelling and Activities
England—De la Mare, Walter. *Molly Whuppie.* New York: Farrar, Straus, Giroux, 1983. Draw a picture and write a sentence.
China—Hong, Lily Toy. "Two of Everything." *Two of Everything: A Chinese Folk Tale.* Morton Grove: Albert Whitman, 1992." Retell the story, dictating into the computer.

Japan—Uchida, Yoshiko. "The Terrible Black Snake's Revenge." *The Sea of Gold and Other Tales from Japan.* New York: Scribner, 1965. 112-20. Sequence strips.

England—Hewitt, Kathryn. *The Three Sillies.* San Diego: Harcourt, 1986. Draw pictures of the beginning, middle, and end of the story.

France—Kimmel, Eric. *The Three Sacks of Truth: A Story from France.* New York: Holiday House, 1993. Mapping activity.

• Choose a Folktale (one whole class session)
  1. Make index cards with call number, author, title–398.2 single edition folktales (see database list).
  2. Whole class in IMC. Bring something quiet to work on.
  3. Explain 398.2, author letter, location in IMC.
  4. Each child picks a card.
  5. Each table goes to 398.2 in turn and children look for books from card.
  6. If they don't like first choice, may choose one other.
  7. Child signs out book for use in classroom.

• Create a Picture Book (Gag, Wanda. *Gone is Gone.* New York: Coward, 1935; or Bang, Molly. *Wiley and the Hairy Man.* New York: Macmillan, 1976.)
  1. In the IMC: Tell the story. Divide the story into scenes. Assign each scene to a student
  2. In the classroom: Students write the narration for their scene
  3. In the IMC: Go through narrations, checking to see that nothing is omitted or put in twice.
  4. In the classroom: Edit and write a final copy.
  5. In the IMC: Type up the pages.
  6. In the classroom: Draw pictures for the pages.
  7. In the IMC: Duplicate the book for each student.

• Battle of the Folktales
Class battles. Then choose six representatives from each room.
Final battle in the IMC. Three teams with two students from each room on each team.

MALORE I. BROWN
Assistant Professor
School of Library and Information Science
University of Wisconsin-Milwaukee

Appendix B
Evaluating Stories for Diverse Audiences: Annotated Bibliography of Research Tools

Aarne, Antti. *The Types of the Folktale: A Classification and Bibliography.* 2nd rev. Trans. Stith Thompson. Helsinki: Academia Scientarum Fennica, 1961.

> A comprehensive classification and internationally accepted method of classifying tales. Tale types are given numbers and categorized.

Eastman, Mary Huse. *Index to Fairy Tales, Myths, and Legends.* 2nd ed. Boston: Faxon, 1926.

> One of the earliest of all title indices to fairy tales for children. Cross-references are given from one story to another, title, and subject.

Ireland, Norma Olin. *Index to Fairy Tales 1949-1972.* Westwood: Faxon, 1973.

> The second supplement to the Eastman *Index* did not list any tales printed after 1948. A new index was issued by Ireland for tales published between 1949 and 1972.

Ireland, Norma Olin and Joseph W. Sprug. *Index to Fairy Tales 1978-1986: Including Folklore, Legends, and Myths in Collections.* 5th Supplement. Metuchen: Scarecrow Press, 1989.

> This series originated as *Index to Fairy Tales, Myths, and Legends* by Mary Huse Eastman. These indexes were begun in 1926 by Eastman and updated periodically by Ireland.

MacDonald, Margaret Read. *The Storyteller's Sourcebook: A Subject, Title, and Motif Index to Folklore Collections for Children.* Detroit: Neal-Schuman/Gale Research, 1982.

> Allows searching by title, subject, and geographical location. Arranged by categories from the Stith Thompson *Motif-Index of Folk-Literature.*

Thompson, Stith. *The Motif-Index of Folk-Literature.* 6 vols. Rev. ed. Bloomington: Indiana University Press, 1955-58.

> A six-volume encyclopedic work which specifically deals with motifs, not tales. Motif, defined by Thompson as "the smallest element of the tales," can be an element, concept, activity, or any detail found in folktales.

Ziegler, Elsie. *Folklore: An Annotated Bibliography and Index to Single Editions.* Westwood, MA: Faxon, 1973.

> Because the Ireland index did not include books consisting of only one tale, this index was prepared by Zeigler to fill the void.

COMPILED BY JANICE M. DEL NEGRO
Editor, *The Bulletin of the Center for Children's Books*
Graduate School of Library and Information Science
University of Illinois at Urbana-Champaign

Appendix C
Allerton Institute 1997
Discography

JANICE HARRINGTON
Janice Harrington, Storyteller. Audiotape. Janice Harrington, 1996.

    Contact: Janice Harrington
              802 S. Prairie
              Champaign, IL 61820

DAN KEDING
Dragons, Giants & the Devil's Hide. Audiotape. Turtle Creek Recordings, 1992.
Promises Kept, Promises Broken. Audiotape. Turtle Creek Recordings, TC 1007, 1995.
South Side Stories. Audiotape. Turtle Creek Recordings, TC 1006, 1993.
Stories from the Other Side. Audiotape. Dan Keding, 1990.

    Contact: Dan Keding
              Turtle Creek Recordings
              P.O. Box 1701
              Springfield, IL 62705

SUSAN KLEIN
Old Standbys. Audiotape. Susan Klein, 1994.
Through a Ruby Window: A Martha's Vineyard Childhood. Audiotape. Susan Klein, 1993.
Wisdom's Tribute. Audiotape. Susan Klein, 1997.

    Contact: Susan Klein
              P.O. Box 214
              Oak Bluffs, MA 02557
              Phone: (508) 693-4140
              Fax: (508) 693-6693
              Web: http://www.susanklein.com

ANNOTATED BY LORETTA GAFFNEY, M.S.
Graduate School of Library and Information Science
University of Illinois at Urbana-Champaign

Appendix D
Resources For Storytellers:
An Annotated Bibliography

Allison, Christine. *I'll Tell You a Story, I'll Sing You a Song: A Parents' Guide to the Fairy Tales, Fables, Songs and Rhymes of Childhood.* New York: Delacorte, 1987. 216 pp.

> A collection of nursery rhymes, fables and songs for use with children. Includes tips about audience, the uses of rhyme in child development, historical background, selection, and performance. A great resource for teachers and librarians, as well as parents.

Baker, Augusta and Ellin Greene. *Storytelling: Art and Technique.* 2nd ed. New York: Bowker, 1987. 182 pp.

> Includes background on the history and theory of storytelling and its purpose in our culture. Reviews steps for the teller in preparing and presenting a story. Includes appendices for planning and promoting festivals and workshops, as well as a bibliography of stories for telling.

Bauer, Caroline Feller. *Caroline Feller Bauer's New Handbook for Storytellers: With Stories, Poems, Magic, and More.* Chicago: ALA, 1993. 550 pp.

> A highly comprehensive sourcebook especially useful for creating storytelling programming—includes tips on promotion, preparing stories, program planning, and incorporating film, music, magic, and word games into programs.

Birch, Carol and Melissa Heckler, eds. *Who Says?: Essays on Pivotal Issues in Contemporary Storytelling.* Little Rock: August House, 1996. 221 pp.

> A collection of essays by prominent storytellers, educators and folklorists addressing key issues in the field of storytelling. Includes essays addressing the problem of "ownership" and folktales, copyright and fair use issues, folktale adaptation, and the role of stories in community life.

Bruchac, Joseph. *Tell Me a Tale: A Book About Storytelling.* San Diego: Harcourt, 1997. 117 pp.

> Veteran storyteller Joseph Bruchac incorporates many of his favorite tales into a discussion of the four basic components of storytelling—listening, observing, remembering, and sharing. Includes a bibliography of resources for the teller.

Dailey, Sheila. *Putting the World in a Nutshell: The Art of the Formula Tale.* Bronx: H.W. Wilson, 1994. 118 pp.

> Tips for choosing and analyzing tales based on their "tale type" or formula, including cumulative tales, chain stories, circle stories, question stories, and more. Also includes notes for researching popular folktale sources and their variants.

De Wit, Dorothy. *Children's Faces Looking Up: Program Building For the Storyteller.* Chicago: ALA, 1979. 156 pp.

> Tips for building storyhours with suggestions for tales, sample story programs, and tips for effective programming. Includes a bibliography of both professional resources and tales for telling.

Geisler, Harlynne. *Storytelling Professionally: The Nuts and Bolts of a Working Performer.* Englewood: Libraries Unlimited, 1997. 151 pp.

> An invaluable resource for anyone wishing to explore the possibilities of professional telling. Includes tips for promotion, research, dealing with copyright issues and more. Emphasizes dealing with potential problems before they occur, including space management, stage fright, and censorship.

Hayes, Joe. *Here Comes the Storyteller.* El Paso: Cinco Puntos Press, 1996. 79 pp.

> Veteran children's storyteller Joe Hayes gives advice about telling using his favorite tales as examples. Special emphasis is given to tone, body language, and engagement with an audience of children.

MacDonald, Margaret Read. *The Storyteller's Start-Up Book: Finding, Learning, Performing, and Using Folktales, Including Twelve Tellable Tales.* Little Rock: August House, 1993. 215 pp.

> This source book begins with an invitation to tell stories, then proceeds to guide the beginning teller through the stages of selecting and learning stories, performance techniques, and sharing tips with other tellers. Includes "twelve tellable tales" that audiences are likely to love, with tips for effective telling. A valuable resource for any storyteller.

Mooney, William and David Holt. *The Storyteller's Guide: Storytellers Share Advice for the Classroom, Boardroom, Showroom, Podium, Pulpit and Center Stage.* Little Rock: August House, 1996. 208 pp.

Includes storytelling tips from some of America's most prominent tellers, including choosing and learning stories, performance techniques, promotion and overcoming stage fright. Readers will enjoy the funny anecdotes—both successes and failures—that the tellers share. Includes a bibliography of resources for tellers.

Painter, William M. *Musical Story Hours: Using Music with Storytelling and Puppetry.* Hamden: Library Professional Publications, 1989. 158 pp.

Tips for incorporating music into storytimes, including a case study, matching music with characters, melodies, holiday programming "off the wall" stories and music and contemporary children's literature, fables, and folktales. Includes a quick reference sections of both tales and music.

Pellowski, Anne. *The Family Storytelling Handbook : How to Use Stories, Anecdotes, Rhymes, Handkerchiefs, Paper, and Other Objects to Enrich Your Family Traditions.* New York: MacMillan, 1987. 150 pp.

Geared toward parents, but useful for anyone who works with storytelling for children. Includes suggestions for storytelling occasions, kinds of stories to tell, tips for telling, and ways to use paper and handkerchiefs in storycrafting. Includes a bibliography of sources and stories for telling, as well as an appendix of storytelling events.

—. *The World of Storytelling.* New York: Bowker, 1977. 296 pp.

Examines the different types of storytelling traditions and their characteristics, including bardic, folk, library, religious, and theatrical traditions. Gives tips for telling based on the style of the tale or storytelling tradition, and an overview of training methods. Includes multilingual dictionary of terms and extensive bibliography of resources and tales for telling.

Sawyer, Ruth. *The Way of the Storyteller.* New York: Viking, 1976. 356 pp.

A classic of storytelling literature. Sawyer provides an account of her development as a teller and the joys and pitfalls she experienced along the way. Includes some of her favorite stories for telling, as well as bibliography of both stories and professional resources.

Sierra, Judy. *The Storyteller's Research Guide: Folktales, Myths, and Legends.* Eugene: Folkprint, 1996. 90 pp.

An invaluable resource for researching popular folktales and their variants. Is also especially useful for tracing the development of myths and legends common to more than one culture.

Shedlock, Marie L. *The Art of the Story-Teller.* 3rd ed. Dover, 1951. 290 pp.

An historical landmark of storytelling, with tips for preparing and telling stories for children. Uses many examples of traditional tales in her advice, and includes a section of questions asked by teachers. Also includes a bibliography of story sources, amplified by Eulalie Steinmetz.

Ziskind, Sylvia. *Telling Stories to Children.* New York: H.W. Wilson, 1976. 162 pp.

> One of the classics of "how to" storytelling manuals—walks the teller through all the stages of working up a story, including selection, learning the story, performance, and programming tips. Includes a bibliography of stories for telling.

JANICE M. DEL NEGRO
Editor, *The Bulletin of the Center for Children's Books*
Graduate School of Library and Information Science
University of Illinois at Urbana-Champaign

Appendix E
Storycrafting: Retelling Old Tales
A Bibliography

Aldana, Patricia. *Jade and Iron: Latin American Tales from Two Cultures.* Toronto: Groundwood-Douglas & McIntyre, 1996.

Bailey, Carolyn. *For the Story Teller: Story Telling and Stories to Tell.* Detroit: Gale, 1975.

Baker, Augusta and Ellin Greene. *Storytelling: Art and Technique.* 2nd ed. New York: Bowker, 1987.

Baltuck, Naomi. *Apples from Heaven: Multicultural Folktales About Stories and Storytellers.* North Haven: Linnet, 1995.

Barton, Bob. *Stories in the Classroom: Storytelling, Reading Aloud, and Roleplaying with Children.* Portsmouth: Heinemann, 1990.

—. *Tell Me Another: Storytelling and Reading Aloud at Home, at School, and in the Community.* Markham: Pembroke, 1986.

Bauer, Caroline Feller. *Handbook for Storytellers.* Chicago: ALA, 1977.

Bauman, Richard. *Verbal Art as Performance.* Prospect Heights: Waveland, 1984.

Bettelheim, Bruno. *The Uses of Enchantment: The Meaning and Importance of Fairy Tales.* New York: Knopf, 1976.

Birch, Carol and Melissa Heckler, eds. *Who Says?: Essays on Pivotal Issues in Contemporary Storytelling.* Little Rock: August House, 1996.

Bottigheimer, Ruth. *Grimms' Bad Girls and Bold Boys: The Moral and Social Vision of the Tales.* New Haven: Yale U P, 1987.

Breneman, Lucille. *Once Upon A Time: A Storytelling Handbook.* Chicago: Nelson-Hall, 1983.

Bruchac, Joseph. *Tell Me a Tale: A Book About Storytelling.* San Diego: Harcourt, 1997.

Bruchac, Joseph and Gayle Ross. *The Girl who Married the Moon: Tales from Native North America.* Mahwah: BridgeWater, 1994.

Bryant, Sara Cone. *How to Tell Stories to Children.* Boston: Houghton, 1979.

Campbell, Joseph. *The Hero With a Thousand Faces.* Princeton: Princeton U P, 1949.

Cassady, Marsh. *Storytelling Step By Step.* San Jose: Resource Publications, 1990.

Cathon, Laura, ed. *Stories to Tell Children: A Selected List.* Pittsburgh: U of Pittsburgh P, 1974.

Clarkson, Atelia and Gilbert B. Cross, eds. *World Folktales.* New York: Scribner, 1980.

Cole, Joanna and Jill Karla Schwarz, eds. *Best-Loved Folktales from Around the World.* Anchor-Doubleday, 1983.

Cooper, Pamela and Rives Collins. *Look What Happened to Frog: Storytelling in Education.* Scottsdale: Gorsuch Scarisbrick, 1992.

Colwell, Eileen. *Storytelling.* London: Bodley Head, 1980.

Cook, Elizabeth. *The Ordinary and the Fabulous: An Introduction to Myths, Legends and Fairytales.* 2nd ed. Cambridge: Cambridge U P, 1976.

Dailey, Sheila. *Putting the World in a Nutshell: The Art of the Formula Tale.* Bronx: H. W. Wilson, 1994.

De Wit, Dorothy. *Children's Faces Looking Up: Program Building for the Storyteller.* Chicago: ALA, 1979.

Dieckmann, Hans. *Twice-Told Tales: The Pyschological Use of Fairy Tales.* Wilmette: Chiron, 1986.

Eastman, Mary. *Index to Fairy Tales, Myths and Legends.* Boston: Boston Books, 1915.

—. *Index to Fairy Tales, Myths and Legends, Second Supplement.* Boston: Faxon, 1952.

Farrell, Catherine. *Effects of Storytelling: An Ancient Art for Modern Classrooms.* San Francisco: Word Weaving, 1982.

—. *Storytelling: A Guide for Teachers.* New York: Scholastic, 1991.

—. *Word Weaving: A Guide to Storytelling.* San Francisco: Zellerbach Family Fund, 1983.

Forest, Heather. *Wisdom Tales from Around the World.* Little Rock: August House, 1996.

Funk and Wagnalls Standard Dictionary of Folklore, Mythology, and Legend. San Francisco: Harper & Row, 1984.

Hamilton, Martha. *Children Tell Stories: A Teaching Guide.* Katonah: R. C. Owen, 1990.

Hamilton, Martha and Mitch Weiss. *Stories in My Pocket: Tales Kids Can Tell.* Golden: Fulcrum, 1996.

Harrell, John. *The Man on a Dolphin: The Storyteller and His Tales.* Kensington: York House, 1983.

—. *Origins and Early Traditions of Storytelling.* Kensington: York House, 1983.

Harrell, John and Mary Harrell, comp. *A Storyteller's Treasury.* Berkeley: Harrell, 1977.

—. *To Tell of Gideon: The Art of Storytelling.* Audiotape. Berkeley: Harrell, 1975.

Ireland, Norma. *Index to Fairy Tales, 1949-1972: Including Folklore, Legends, and Myths in Collections.* Westwood: Faxon, 1973.

—. *Index to Fairy Tales, 1973-1977: Including Folklore, Legends, and Myths in Collections.* Metuchen: Scarecrow, 1985.

Lipman, Doug. *The Storytelling Coach: How to Listen, Praise, and Bring Out People's Best.* Little Rock: August House, 1995.

Livo, Norma. *Storytelling Activities.* Englewood: Libraries Unlimited, 1987.

—. *Storytelling Folklore Sourcebook.* Englewood: Libraries Unlimited, 1991.

—. *Storytelling: Process and Practice.* Littleton: Libraries Unlimited, 1986.

—. *Troubadour's Storybag: Musical Folktales of the World.* Golden: Fulcrum, 1996.

Livo, Norma and Dia Cha. *Folk Stories of the Hmong: People of Laos, Thailand, and Vietnam.* Englewood: Libraries Unlimited, 1991.

Luthi, Max. *Once Upon a Time: On the Nature of Fairy Tales.* Bloomington: Indiana U P, 1976.

—. *The European Folktale: Form and Nature.* Bloomington: Indiana U P, 1986.

—. *The Fairytale as Art Form and Portrait of Man.* Bloomington: Indiana U P, 1987.

MacDonald, Margaret Read. *Look Back and See: Twenty Lively Tales for Gentle Tellers.* New York: H.W. Wilson, 1991.

—. *The Parent's Guide to Storytelling: How to Make Up New Stories and Retell Old Favorites.* New York: HarperCollins, 1995.

—. *The Storyteller's Sourcebook: A Subject, Title, and Motif Index to Folklore Collections for Children.* Detroit: Gale, 1982.

—. *The Storyteller's Start-Up Book: Finding, Learning, Performing, and Using Folktales, Including Twelve Tellable Tales.* Little Rock: August House, 1993.

—. *Twenty Tellable Tales: Audience Participation Folktales for the Beginning Storyteller.* New York: H.W. Wilson, 1988.

—. *When the Lights Go Out: Twenty Scary Tales to Tell.* Bronx: H.W. Wilson, 1988.

Maguire, Jack. *Creative Storytelling: Choosing, Inventing, and Sharing Tales for Children.* New York: McGraw-Hill, 1985.

Martin, Rafe. *The Hungry Tigress: Buddhist Legends and Jataka Tales.* Berkeley: Parallax, 1990.

—. *Mysterious Tales of Japan.* New York: Putnam's, 1996.

Mason, Harriet. *Every One a Storyteller: Integrating Storytelling into the Curriculum.* Portland: Lariat, 1991.

May, Rollo. *The Cry for Myth.* New York: Norton, 1991.

Mayo, Margaret. *Mythical Birds and Beasts from Many Lands.* New York: Dutton, 1997.

—. *Magical Tales from Many Lands.* New York: Dutton, 1993.

McCaughrean, Geraldine. *The Silver Treasure: Myths and Legends of the World.* New York: M. K. McElderry, 1997.

—. *The Golden Hoard: Myths and Legends.* New York: M. K. McElderry, 1996.

Moore, Robin. *Awakening the Hidden Storyteller.* Boston: Shambhala, 1991.

Opie, Iona Archibald and Peter Opie, comp. *The Classic Fairy Tales.* London: Oxford U P, 1974.

Pellowski, Anne. *The World of Storytelling.* New York: Bowker, 1977.

Powers, Effie. *Bag O' Tales: A Source Book for Story-Tellers.* New York: Dutton, 1934.

Propp, Vladimir. *Theory and History of Folklore.* Minneapolis: U of Minnesota P, 1984.

Ross, Ramon Royal. *Storyteller: The Classic that Heralded America's Storytelling Revival.* 3rd rev. ed. Little Rock: August House, 1996.

Rugoff, Milton, ed. *A Harvest of World Folk Tales.* New York: Viking, 1949.

San Souci, Robert. *Cut from the Same Cloth: American Women of Myth, Legend, and Tall Tale.* New York: Philomel, 1993.

Sawyer, Ruth. *The Way of the Storyteller:* New York: Viking, 1942.

Schimmel, Nancy. *Just Enough to Make a Story: A Sourcebook for Storytelling.* 3rd ed. Berkeley: Sister's Choice, 1992.

Scott, Edna Lyman. *Story Telling: What to Tell and How to Tell It.* Detroit: Singing Tree Press, 1971.

Shedlock, Marie. *The Art of the Story-Teller.* New York: Dover, 1951.

Sherman, Josepha. *Trickster Tales: Forty Folk Stories from Around the World.* Little Rock: August House, 1996.

Sierra, Judy. *Twice Upon A Time: Stories to Tell, Retell, Act Out, and Write About.* Bronx: H.W. Wilson, 1989.

Thompson, Stith. *One Hundred Favorite Folktales.* Bloomington: Indiana University Press, 1968.

Tooze, Ruth. *Storytelling.* Englewood Cliffs: Prentice-Hall, 1959.

Vivian, Francis. *Story-Weaving: A Text-Book on the Craft of Story-Writing.* London: Hutchinson's Scientific & Technical Pub., 1940.

Wilson, Jane. *The Story Experience.* Metuchen: Scarecrow, 1979.

Yolen, Jane, ed. *Favorite Folktales from Around the World.* New York: Pantheon, 1986.

Zipes, Jack. *Breaking the Magic Spell: Radical Theories of Folk and Fairy Tales.* New York: Methuen, 1984.

—. *Don't Bet On the Prince: Contemporary Feminist Fairy Tales in North America and England.* New York: Methuen, 1986.

—. *Fairy Tales and the Art of Subversion: The Classical Genre for Children and the Process of Civilization.* New York: Wildman, 1983.

—. *The Trials and Tribulations of Little Red Riding Hood: Versions of the Tale in Sociocultural Context.* South Hadley: Bergin and Garvey, 1983.

Ziskind, Sylvia. *Telling Stories to Children.* New York: H.W. Wilson, 1976.

About the Contributors

MALORE I. BROWN is an assistant professor at the Graduate School of Library and Information Science at the University of Wisconsin-Milwaukee, where she teachers courses in multicultural literature for youth, school library media services, and children's and young adult materials and services. She is past president of the Wisconsin Black Librarians Network, and has served on the Association for Library Services to Children Selection of Children's Books and Materials from Various Cultures Committee for the American Library Association. Brown's articles have appeared in *Culture Keepers II: Proceedings of the 2nd National Conference of African American Librarians* (Faxon 1995), and *In Our Own Voices: The Changing Face of Librarianship* (Scarecrow 1996).

JANICE M. DEL NEGRO is the editor of the *The Bulletin of the Center for Children's Books* at the Graduate School of Library and Information Science, University of Illinois at Urbana-Champaign. Prior to coming to *The Bulletin* she was a consultant for children's and public library services for the State Library of North Carolina, and she worked for 14 years as a children's librarian for the Chicago Public Library, including five years as assistant director of Systemwide Children's Services. Del Negro has taught storytelling at Dominican College and the University of Illinois. She has also taught children's library services at Dominican College; presented workshops on storytelling nationally; and been a reviewer for *Booklist*, *School Library Journal*, and *Kirkus Reviews*. An active member of the American Library Association, Del Negro has served on both the Newbery and Caldecott committees. She is the author of *Lucy Dove*, published by DK Ink in Fall 1998.

JANICE HARRINGTON is the head of Youth Services for the Champaign Public Library in Champaign, Illinois. An accomplished storyteller, Harrington has been a featured teller at the Illinois Storytelling Festival, the National

Storytelling Festival in Jonesborough, Tennesee, and the National Festival of Black Storytelling. She is a member of the American Library Association and served on the 1999 Caldecott Committee for the Association for Library Services to Children. Harrington has been a guest reviewer for *The Bulletin of the Center for Children's Books*, and has given workshops on storytelling and multicultural literature. Her first audiotape, *Janice Harrington, Storyteller*, was produced in 1996.

BETSY HEARNE teaches children's literature and storytelling in the Graduate School of Library and Information Science at the University of Illinois, Urbana-Champaign. A former children's book review editor for *Booklist* and *The Bulletin of the Center for Childrens Books*, she has lectured and written widely on children's books and folklore. Hearne's articles include "Patterns of Sound, Sight, and Story: From Literature to Literacy," and "Disney Revisited: Or Jiminy Cricket, It's Musty Down Here!" She is the author of *Choosing Books for Children: A Commonsense Guide* and *Beauty and the Beast: Visions and Revisions of an Old Tale*, and the editor of several other books. In addition, Hearne has published five novels for children, two collections of poetry for young adults, and the critically acclaimed picture book *Seven Brave Women*.

CHRISTINE JENKINS is an assistant professor at the Graduate School of Library and Information Science, University of Illinois at Urbana-Champaign, where she teaches courses in youth services, young adult literature, gender issues, and LIS foundations and history. Her work has appeared in *Library Quarterly, Libraries and Culture, Journal of Youth Services in Libraries, Booklist, Feminist Collections*, and *Reclaiming the American Library Past: Writing the Women In* (Ablex 1996). She is an active member of the American Library Association in the area of youth services and intellectual freedom, having served on the 1989 Caldecott Committee and as a director of the Intellectual Freedom Round Table and chair of the ALSC Intellectual Freedom Committee.

DAN KEDING is an internationally recognized storyteller and balladeer who has been a featured teller at the National Storytelling Festival in Jonesborough, Tennessee; the Sidmouth International Folk Arts Festival in Sidmouth, England; and the Illinois Storytelling Festival, to name just a few. His love for stories goes beyond performance and into research, resulting in a master's degree from the University of Illinois at Springfield in the history and performance of traditional storytelling and ballads. His audiotape, *Stories from the Other Side*, was selected for the American Library Association's publication, *Best of the Best for Children*.

SUSAN KLEIN is a freelance storyteller from Martha's Vineyard, Massachusetts. She is the founding director and current artistic director of the Festival of Storytelling on Martha's Vineyard, and the author of the autobiographical title, *Through a Ruby Window*. A powerful speaker, Klein is noted for her keynote and inspirational speeches, and her groundbreaking work with adolescents and storytelling. She has been the featured teller at more than 50 storytelling festivals, and three of her audio-cassettes have been award-winners. Her new cassette of rites of passage stories, *Forbidden*, is available in fall 1998; see the Web site www.susanklein.com for more information.

KAREN MORGAN is an instructor at the Graduate School of Library and Information Studies at Texas Woman's University, where she teaches courses in storytelling, library materials for children, and juvenile literature. She is founder of Texas Woman's University STORYTELL listserv, president of the Tejas Storytelling Association, and director of the 1998 Texas Storytelling Festival. Morgan chaired the panel on "Effective Outreach Programming for Young Adults" at the American Library Association's 1996 Annual Conference, and has presented widely at state and regional library and reading conferences. Morgan has reviewed for *The ALAN Review* and is currently a reviewer for *Booklist Books for Youth*.

JUDITH O'MALLEY is the editor of *Book Links: Connecting Books, Libraries, and Classrooms*, a journal intended for school library media specialists, teachers, public children's librarians, and parents who are concerned about connecting high quality trade children's books with the education curriculum. Before assuming the position of *Book Links* editor in November 1996, she worked for seven years as associate editor for The H.W. Wilson Company, where she handled acquisitions and editorial development of all professional books for children's librarians and teachers. Among the books O'Malley worked on in that capacity is the forthcoming *Radical Change: Literature for Youth in an Electronic Age* by Eliza T. Dresang. O'Malley has also written articles for professional and trade journals, including *Wilson Library Bulletin* and *Booklist*.

ANNE SHIMOJIMA is the school library media specialist at Braeside School in Highland Park, Illinois, and brings 25 years of professional experience to the Allerton conference. She has delighted audiences of all ages with her graceful and spirited tellings of folktales from around the world—Asian stories, Jack tales, stories of humor, and stories of the heart. Shimojima has taught storytelling courses for National-Louis University, was on the board of directors of The Wild Onion Storytelling Celebration, and is one of a panel of reviewers for *The Bulletin Storytelling Review*, to be published by the University of Illinois Graduate School of Library and Information Science in 1998.

JOSEPH DANIEL SOBOL has worked as a professional storyteller, musician, and folklorist since 1981; he received a master's degree in folklore from the University of North Carolina and a Ph.D. in Performance Studies from Northwestern University. Sobol's writing on traditional and contemporary storytelling has been published in such journals as *Oral Tradition, Journal of American Folklore,* and the *National Storytelling Journal.* From 1994 to 1998, he toured the United States with "In the Deep Heart's Core," an award-winning original musical theater piece based on the life and poetry of William Butler Yeats. Sobol currently teaches storytelling and folklore at DePaul University School for New Learning. His most recent book, *The Storyteller's Journey: An American Revival,* is to be published by the University of Illinois Press in 1999.

DEBORAH STEVENSON has been with *The Bulletin of the Center for Children's Books* since 1989 and currently holds the position of associate editor. She is a Ph.D. candidate in the English Department of the University of Chicago, where she is currently completing her dissertation on children's literature and contemporary culture. She has taught the history of children's literature at the University of Illinois, and children's literature at Indiana University Northwest and in the continuing education program at the University of Chicago. Stevenson has presented at national and international conferences on children's literature, including The International Research Society for Children's Literature Congress, and her articles have appeared in the *Horn Book Magazine,* the *Lion and the Unicorn,* and the *Children's Literature Association Quarterly.*

BY JENNIFER YOUNG, M. S.
Graduate School of Library and Information Science
University of Illinois at Urbana-Champaign

Index

Aarne, Antti, 54
Adedjouma, Davida, 63
African tales, 55, 57, 59
Alderson, Brian, 46
Alphabet books, 71
Anancy tales, 56-57
Angela's Ashes, 61
Angry Moon, The, 89
Animals: as tricksters, 55
AskEric InfoGuide: Folk and Fairy Tales (website), 16; URL, 18
Audiotapes, 125

Baker, Augusta, 47
Ballard, Martha, 37-39, 41-42, 48
Bannerman, Helen, 53
"Battle of the Folktales," 9
Becoming Rosemary, 39, 48
Bettelheim, Bruno, 46
Bobbsey Twins and Their Schoolmates, The, 85
Brentano, Clemens, 87
Brothers Grimm, The, 86-88
Brown, Malore, 1, 22; biography, 135
Brown, Margaret Wise, 67
Bruchac, Joseph, 63
Bryant, Sara Cone, 47
Burden of Dreams, 81
Butler, Dorothy, 71

Campbell, Joseph, 24
Cantwell, Robert, 32
Changeover, The, 39
Chaplin, Charlie, 73
Chester Inn, 29
Children's librarianship, 45-49, 84-86, 98-105
Children's literature, 44-46, 48; knowledge of, 102-104; marketing of, 85-86, 88, 90; popular culture, 90-91; series, 85, 90
Children's Literature Web Guide, The (website), 16; URL, 18
Chodorow, Nancy, 48
Christie, Gregory, 63
Christopher Taylor cabin, 29
Cinderella: classroom activities, 8; variants, 16, 118-119
Civic Trust. *See* Jonesborough Civic Trust
Classroom activities: *Cinderella*, 8; fairy tales, 8; family stories, 17; folktales, 8, 120-122; mythology/astronomy, 9; Native Americans, 9-10; video stories, 9
Collins, Meghan, 40
Colwell, Eileen, 47, 97
Cooper, Ilene, 62
Corporate mergers, 91-92

Cottingley fairy incident, 70
Countess from Hong Kong, A, 73
Creed, Robert, 31
Cuevas, Lou, 52
Cultural heritage, 7

Damessae, Selashe, 31
Das Baul, Purna, 31
Davis, Don: *Smithsonian Magazine* (website), 11
Davis, Mary Gould, 47
Dead Sea Scrolls, The, 62
Del Negro, Janice, 1-2, 83, 106; biography, 135; website, 17; workshop, 20
"Developing Student Voices on the Internet," 63
Doyle, Arthur Conan, 70
Dresang, Eliza, 63
Dusinberre, Juliet, 71

Easter Bunny That Overslept, The, 69
Eastman, Mary Huse, 54
Egielski, Richard, 67
Elderbarry's Storytelling Home Page (website), 17; URL, 19
Ellerbee, Linda, 73
Ellis, Sarah, 72
Encyclopedia Mythica, The (website), 16; URL, 19
End of the Rainbow, The, 72
English Boy's Magazine, The, 46
Etcher's Studio, The, 81; illustration, 82
European tales, 55
Everett, Gwen, 75

Family secrets, 61-62
Family storytelling: bibliography, 113-114
Family tales, 61-62, 64; websites, 17
"fis phenomenon," 70
Fiske, John, 90, 92
FOLKLORE (listserv), 12
Folklorists: respect of, 47-48

Folktales: altering of, 89; classroom activities, 8, 120-122; mythology, 55; nationalistic traditions, 87
Forest, Heather, 32
Friedrich, Otto, 69
Friedrich, Priscilla, 69
Furlong, Monica, 39

Geisert, Arthur, 1-2, 60, 78, 81; illustrations, 79-80, 82
Gender and the Academic Experience, 48
Ghost tales, 34, 59
Gilligan, Carol, 48
Gillman, Jackson, 32
Going Back Home, 75
Goldsmith, Evelyn, 70
Grandmother Bryant's Pocket, 72
Gray, Spalding, 31
Great Building Saga, 78
"Green Woman, The," 40
Greene, Ellin, 5
Grimm Brothers, 86-88
Grimm, Jacob, 86-88
Grimm, Wilhelm, 86-88
Groff, Patrick, 73

Halloween costumes, 92-94
Hammerstein, Oscar, 70, 75
Hannigan, Jane Anne, 45
Harrington, Janice, 1, 59; audiotapes, 125; biography, 135-136
Hawthorne, Nathaniel, 43
Hazard, Paul, 85
Hearne, Betsy, 1, 22, 54; biography, 135; Sleeping Beauty, 90; slides, 69
Hepburn, Katharine, 73
Hero-journey cycle, 44-45
Hicks, Ray, 32-33
Hicks, Rosa, 32-33
"How to Get Your Ph.D. in Children's Literature," 46
Huck, Charlotte, 89
Hyman, Trina Schart, 74

INDEX

Igus, Toyomi, 75
Index to Fairy Tales, 54
Indexes, 123-124
Internet resources: listervs, 11-15; search engines, 15-16; URLs, 18-19, 117; Usenet newsgroups, 12; websites, 11-17, 63
Ireland, Norma Olin, 54

Jack tales, 9, 32-33; bibliography, 119
"Jeaning of America, The," 90
Jenkins, Christine, 1, 45, 74, 83; biography, 136
"Johnny, We Hardly Knew Ye," 59
Johnston, Tony, 67
Jonesborough, Tennessee, 23; Chester Inn, 29; Christopher Taylor cabin, 29-30 ; Swappin' Grounds, 29-30, 32
Jonesborough Civic Trust, 23

Kane, Alice, 31
Keding, Dan, 1, 59; audiotapes, 125; biography, 136
KidsCom (website), 63; URL, 65
Kimmel, Eric, 67
KISS (Keep it simple, stupid), 20
Klein, Susan, 1, 59; audiotapes, 125; biography, 136-137; workshop, 20-21

Language skills: improvement, 6
Larkin, Chuck, 17
Lauper, Cyndi, 84
Legends: traditional telling of, 52
Lester, Julius, 53
Library advocacy, 98-105
Library Services for Children, 84, 97
Li'l Sis and Uncle Willie, 75
Lipman, Doug (website), 17; URL, 19
Listening skills: improvement, 6
Lundin, Anne, 45

MacDonald, Margaret Read, 54

Magic Circle, The, 39
Mahy, Margaret, 39
Marcellino, Fred, 53
Marcus, Leonard, 71
Martin, Connie, 31
Martin, Rafe, 28
Marx, Karl, 84
McConnell, Doc, 29-30, 33; and Crazy Jim, 30
McCourt, Frank, 61
McWilliam, Barry (website), 17; URL, 19
Michelet, Jules, 38
Midwife's Apprentice, The, 39, 48
Midwife's Tale, A, 37
Midwives: archetypes, 39; community of, 48; diaries, 37-38; as healers, 40-42; history, 37-38; and magic, 41, 44; as mentors, 39-40; perceptions, 38; sexuality, 40; spinning/weaving, 41
Minnich, Elizabeth, 48
Morgan, Karen: 1, 3; biography, 137
Most Popular Web Sites: The Best of the Net from A2Z, 16
"Mr. Fox" (story), 6-7
"Multicultural Literature for Children and Young Adults," 52
Myths, 24, 55
Mythology/Astronomy: classroom activities, 9

Nadel, Miriam, 17
Naftali the Storyteller and His Horse, Sus, and Other Stories, 4
National Storytelling Festival: 116-117; analysis, 23-26; programs, 31-32; the experience, 26-35; travel to, 27-30; workshops, 31-32
Native Americans: classroom activities, 9-10; tales, 55
Nickerson, Ken, 18
Nodelman, Perry, 66, 68, 71, 73, 76

Nursery and Household Tales (Kinder- und Haus-Märchen), 87-88

O'Malley, Judith, 1, 60; biography, 137
Olio, 31
Organizations, 116-117
Ortiz, Simon, 31

Palm of My Heart: Poetry by African American Children, The, 63
Periodicals: bibliography, 116
Picture books: adaptations, 75; authors, 67; book smells, 71; children's reactions, 71; creation of, 8-9; illustrations, 68-69; impact, 72; narratives, 66-70; online environment, 74; physical format, 71-72; synthesis of forms, 72-76; technical aspects, 69; text, 67-68
Pigs From 1 to 10, 78; illustration, 79
Pigs From A to Z, 78; illustration, 80
"Pied Piper's New Melodies: Folktale Variations, The," 62-63
Pinkney, Jerry, 53
Poarch, Margaret, 98
Pocket Book of Verse, The, 96
Potter, Beatrix, 72
Pourquoi tales. *See* African tales
Power, Effie L., 84-85, 97, 98
Presser, Harriet, 48
Princess Furball, 89
Propp, Vladmir, 24
Publishing: involvement of women, 42-44
Purkiss, Diane, 44

Reader's theater, 17
Real Thing, The, 76
"Recent Storytelling Titles" (website), 17
Resources, 54; bibliography, 126-129
Reuter, Bjarne, 72

Revival story, 25
Root, Mary E.S., 85
Rubright, Lynn, 31

Sacred tales, 35
Sam and the Tigers, 53
San Souci, Robert, 67
Sawyer, Ruth, 47, 104-105
School library media centers, 4-10; bibliography, 108-122
Schram, Penninah, 31
Schwarcz, Joseph, 73
Scieszka, Jon, 67
Sendak, Maurice, 67, 71-73
Shannon, George, 23-24, 62
Shedlock, Marie, 47
Shimojima, Anne: 1, 3; biography, 137
Sima, Judy, 63
Simms, Laura, 32
Singer, Isaac Bashevis, 4
Sixties, The (website), 17; URL, 19
Sleator, William, 89
Smith, Jimmy Neil, 23
Smith, Lane, 67
Smith, Mary Carter, 31
Smithsonian Magazine: website, 11; URL, 19
Snake Book, The, 72
Snow White, 90; website, 16; URL, 19
Sobol, Joseph Daniel, 1-2, 22, 106; biography, 137-138
Sondheim, Stephen, 74-75
Southern Folklife Collection (website), 16; URL, 19
Speare, Elizabeth, 39
Spelman, Jon, 32
Spiritual nurturing, 5
Statue of Liberty, 70
Stevenson, Deborah, 1, 60; biography, 138
Stoppard, Tom, 76
"Story-Enhancing Your Science Lessons," 63
Story of Little Babaji, The, 53

Story of Little Black Sambo, The: 22; discussion of, 52-53; variants, 53-54
Story sources: 53-54, 57; evaluation of, 55; websites, 16-19
Storycrafting, 130-134
"Storycrafting: Retelling Traditional Tales," 20
STORYTELL: archives, 18; discussions, 13-15; listserv, 11-12, 14; makeup, 13; subscription information, 117
Storytelling: Art & Technique, 5
Storytelling community, 25
Storytelling: exclusion of women, 42-43; future of, 83, 106-107
Storytelling patterns, 24
Storytelling practice, 3, 7-10; 20
Storytelling ring (webring), 17-18
Storytelling Sourcebook, The, 54
"Suitable for children," 88-90
Sutcliff, Rosemary, 39

"Talk," 59
Tall tales, 55
Tatar, Maria, 87-88
Taylor, Edgar, 88
Teacher-student relationships, 5-6
Teaching: bibliography, 114; using stories, 8-9, 17, 52-57
"Telling Family Stories" (website), 17; URL, 19
"Tiger's Minister of State," 59
Thompson, Stith, 57
Thorne-Thompsen, Gudrun, 47
Throgs Neck Branch (NYPL), 97
Tooze, Ruth, 47
Torrence, Jackie, 34
Turner, Victor, 24, 26
"Turtle's Race with Bear," 63
Tyler, Anna Cogswell, 47
Types of the Folktale, The, 54

Ulrich, Laurel, 37, 39, 42
Understanding Popular Culture, 90

Ungerer, Tomi, 73
Urban legends: bibliography, 114
Uses of Enchantment, The, 47
Usenet newsgroups, 12

Vandergrift, Kay, 16, 45
Van Gennep, Arnold, 26
Vietnam War History Page, The (website), 17; URL, 19
Visit to Williem Blake's Inn, A, 67

Way of the Storyteller, The, 104-105
Web resources. *See* Internet resources.
Where the Wild Things Are, 67-68, 71, 73-74
Whuppie, Molly, 47
Why tales. *See* African tales
Willard, Nancy, 67
Witch of Blackbird Pond, The, 39, 48
Witch's Brat, The, 39
Witches: and midwives, 38-40, 44-45
Witchcraft, Sorcery, and Superstition, 38
Women's studies programs, 48
Wonder tales, 24, 33
Words About Pictures, 68, 71
Workshops, 20-21

Yarnspinner, The, 23
Yorinks, Arthur, 67
"Young Adults, Storytelling, and Rites of Passage," 20
Youth Services librarianship. *See* Children's librarianship.
Youth's Wonderhorn, The (Des Knaben Wunderhorn), 87

Zipes, Jack, 46-47

The Publications Office of the Graduate School of Library and Information Science at the University of Illinois at Urbana-Champaign produces a variety of scholarly and practical publications for library and information science professionals. The office's catalog includes subscription journals, books, conference proceedings and monograph series.
For more information, contact

The Graduate School of Library and Information Science
University of Illinois at Urbana-Champaign
501 E. Daniel St.
Champaign, IL 61820
Voice: (217) 333-1359
Fax: (217) 244-7329
E-mail: puboff@alexia.lis.uiuc.edu
World Wide Web: http://edfu.lis.uiuc.edu/puboff

———— ❖ ————

Consistently ranked as one of the top three library and information science programs in the U. S., the Graduate School of Library and Information Science, founded in 1893 at the Armour Institute in Chicago, maintains a reputation of excellence and quality. The University of Illinois at Urbana-Champaign was founded in 1867, and is regularly cited among leading universities in the United States.